OFF THE BEATEN PATH

OFF THE BEATEN PATH

A Hiking Guide
to
Vancouver's North Shore

Norman D. Watt

HARBOUR PUBLISHING

1 2 3 4 5 — 14 13 12 11 10

Harbour Publishing Co. Ltd.
P.O. Box 219, Madeira Park, BC, V0N 2H0
www.harbourpublishing.com

Cover photograph of hikers on Howe
Sound Crest Trail by Khaled Ben-Rabha
Edited by Margaret Tessman
Maps by John Lightfoot
Printed and bound in Canada

Harbour Publishing acknowledges financial support from the Government of Canada through the Book Publishing Industry Development Program and the Canada Council for the Arts, and from the Province of British Columbia through the BC Arts Council and the Book Publishing Tax Credit.

Caution: Every effort has been made to ensure the reader's awareness of the hazards and level of expertise involved in the activities in this book, but your own safety is ultimately up to you. The author and publisher take no responsibility for loss or injury incurred by anyone using this book.

Library and Archives Canada Cataloguing in Publication

Watt, Norman D., 1944–
Off the beaten path : a hiking guide to Vancouver's North Shore / Norman D. Watt.

ISBN 978-1-55017-479-3

1. Hiking—British Columbia—North Vancouver—Guidebooks. 2. Hiking—British Columbia—West Vancouver—Guidebooks.   3. Trails—British Columbia—North Vancouver—Guidebooks. 4. Trails—British Columbia—West Vancouver—Guidebooks. 5. North Vancouver (B.C.)—Guidebooks. 6. West Vancouver (B.C.)—Guidebooks. I. Title.

GV199.44.C22B75 2010   796.5109711'33   C2010-900041-2

This book is dedicated to my son Geoffrey and daughter Stephanie, who both grew up on the North Shore of Metro Vancouver.
I hope this book will help them get as much enjoyment as I have had, exploring the great outdoors right here in our own backyard.

Contents

North Vancouver

Addendum

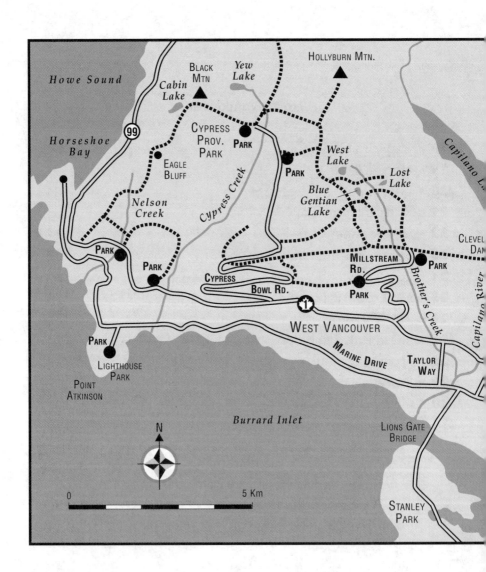

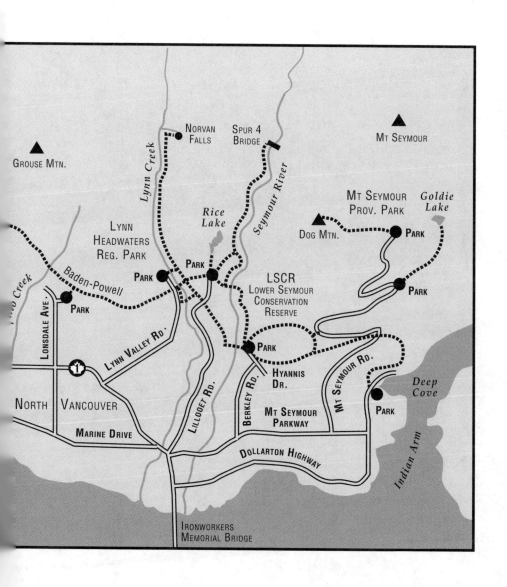

INTRODUCTION

The genesis of this book was back in January 2008, when I first came up with the idea of writing descriptions of some North and West Vancouver hiking trails that I had come to know so well over a period of years. I approached the local newspapers with the idea of a hiking column featuring some of this area's lesser-known trails. The *North Shore News* agreed to run the column during July and August 2008 and "Off the Beaten Path" was born.

Expanding these initial articles and adding enough new ones to make a book seemed to be a logical next step. I began the book project in fall 2008, along with writing new articles for the summer 2009 hiking column, which was also carried by the *North Shore News*. This book consists of 21 hike descriptions from those newspaper columns, all expanded with more detail, including trail maps and photographs, in addition to another 10 new ones not previously published in the newspaper.

The book's focus is on hiking trails through the wilderness of the North Shore forests of Metro Vancouver. As its title implies, this book is unique in that for the most part, these are lesser-known but interesting trails that people may not have seen before in other hiking books. Many of them feature sites of local historical interest, such as early 1900s' logging, homesteading or sporting activities, which are not often found in other hiking books. The level of detail, including thorough trail descriptions and approximate walking times throughout the hikes, also makes this book a distinctive and invaluable resource for the hiker.

There is much here to offer the seasoned outdoor adventurer as well as the casual hiker. With a total of 31 North Shore hikes (15 West Vancouver and 16 North Vancouver), this is the most comprehensive collection of North Shore hiking trails to be found in any hiking book. The remarkable, 48-kilometre Baden-Powell trail that stretches from one end of the North Shore to the other has its own complete section, divided into four manageable segments. Portions of the Baden-Powell trail are also included in many of the other hikes in the West Vancouver and North Vancouver sections.

There is no particular logic to the order of the hikes in this book, other than they are sequenced roughly west to east in each of the three sections.

Trail Information

This book is intended for hikers of all ability levels. A range of estimated timings is provided for each hike to allow for differences in individual walking pace, depending on energy and fitness levels. While the hike could be completed in less time than the low end of the range, the upper end is intended to be generous enough to provide adequate time for most hikers. These hikes, with the exception of the four Baden-Powell segments, are generally less than four hours. The durations noted do not include time for a lunch stop, unless otherwise specified.

Elevation gains are generally the difference between the hike's lowest point (not necessarily the trailhead) and its highest point. They can be used as a good measure of a hike's suitability for you, although they are not cumulative! The 1:50,000 series of federal government topographical maps, available at International Travel Maps and Books, 530 West Broadway in Vancouver (604-879-3621), or at Mountain Equipment Co-op, 1341 Main Street in North Vancouver (604-990-4417), may also be helpful to illustrate the area's topography, although these maps do not include the hiking trails.

While almost all of these hikes are dog-friendly, many of them have signs posted requiring dogs to be on-leash in certain areas.

The season designations are intended to be a general guide to the most appropriate time of year for hiking the trails. You should, however take into account the effect of current weather conditions.

For example, heavy rainfall can turn some trails into creek beds, while unusually heavy snowfall, such as that experienced in the winter of 2008–09, can make even some lower elevation trails difficult to navigate until much later in the spring than usual. High winds at any time of year can bring down trees that will block a trail for extended periods of time.

Although every effort has been made to ensure that these hike descriptions are accurate at time of writing, trails are often altered from one year to the next for various reasons. All of the hikes in this book have been travelled between January and October 2009. Also, the West Vancouver hike descriptions do reflect the changes made to routes and trailheads for the 2009 Highway 1/99 Eagleridge Bypass project and the 2010 Olympics-related construction on Cypress Mountain.

Transportation

Most of these hikes are accessible by public transit. Translink's customer information number is 604-953-3333. Their website, www. translink.bc.ca, provides a Trip Planner, where you can enter your departure point and destination to get bus schedule and route information, including a map. Where applicable I have noted the hikes where private vehicle transportation is required.

Hiking Safety

Hiking does involve an element of risk, and you should take the appropriate steps to ensure your own safety. In addition to your fitness and experience levels, consider external factors such as mountain conditions (wet, slippery, icy trails) and the weather (heat, fog, heavy rainfall, snow, etc.). Even familiar trails look very different under a blanket of snow, and it is easy to go astray when you cannot see the path beneath your feet.

Note the number of daylight hours left before embarking on any hike, and leave yourselves a generous amount of daylight time, particularly if you are unfamiliar with the area. Lack of light is the single most common cause of overdue hiker calls to North Shore Rescue.

The following safety information is provided courtesy of North Shore Rescue. It is summarized with permission from its website, where additional detail is available: www.northshorerescue.com/education.html.

What to Bring—The Ten Essentials

Even the best weather can change rapidly, and even the widest trail can be lost. It pays to take a little extra with you, just in case. North Shore Rescue recommends taking the following:

1. Flashlight or a headlamp with extra batteries and light bulb. Green Cyalume light stick as emergency backup.

2. Whistle (such as the Fox 40 whistle with a lanyard).

3. Matches (waterproof or in plastic bag) or lighter. Also a fire-starter and/or a candle.

4. Extra clothes, hat or toque, gloves or mittens, fleece jacket, Gore-Tex jacket, polypro underwear, good quality hiking socks and Gore-Tex overpants.

5. Pocketknife with quality cutting blade. Can saw (optional).

6. Large orange plastic bag and thermal tarp.

7. Water (Gatorade crystals recommended) and food (high-energy food bars).

8. First-aid kit: Should include pocket mask, Sam Splint, bulk dressings, protective gloves, bandages, scissors and blister dressings.

9. Navigation: Good quality compass with built-in declination adjustment and both topographical and interpretive maps. Also a GPS unit, as an adjunct to compass and map.

10. Communications: Bring a celtel with two fresh batteries and also consider purchasing a two-way radio system called FRS.

Ways to Avoid Becoming Lost
& What to Do if You Do Become Lost

If you get lost today, will anyone know? Are you prepared?

- Leave a message with a friend. A note, left with a responsible person, explains your destination, the route you are taking, who is with you and your return time.

- Always carry the 10 essentials. Be ready to stay out overnight in a survival situation. Carry extra clothing, survival gear and be mentally prepared to endure the night out.

- Never hike alone. Hike with a group and keep together. If a person becomes separated by going ahead or falling behind, they are more likely to become lost.
- Be physically prepared and fit enough to enjoy your chosen hike. Stick to a turn-around time and leave enough time to get home without causing people to worry about you. Take the proper equipment and have a trip plan.
- Do not panic. Maintain a positive mental attitude if you become lost. Being lost is not dangerous if you are prepared.
- Stay where you are. People who go on after becoming lost usually get farther from the trail and farther from people who are looking for them. Help will come.
- Do not go "downhill." On the North Shore, going downhill often leads to dangerous natural drainages. These drainages have the common features of very thick bush, steep cliffs and waterfalls.
- Use signalling devices. Blowing a whistle, lighting a fire and staying visible will help searchers find you. Help people trying to find you, even if you feel embarrassed or afraid. Animals will not be attracted to your signals.
- Build or seek shelter. Protect yourself from the elements. Be as comfortable as possible, but when it is light make sure you are visible to searchers in helicopters or planes.

It could happen to you. Bad weather, early darkness or an unexpected injury can turn an easy hike into an extended crisis. By being prepared you will enjoy your trip in the backcountry regardless of what nature throws at you.

The lighthouse at Point Atkinson in Lighthouse Park.

WEST VANCOUVER

1 ▸ Lighthouse Park

Elevation gain: minimal
High point: 115 metres (380 feet)
Season: Year-round
Topographical map: North Vancouver 92G06
Hiking time: 2 to 2.5 hours
Dog-friendly

Here is a year-round, energetic outing to a national historic site with rewarding views across both Burrard Inlet and Howe Sound as you roam through Metro Vancouver's last stand of rugged, old-growth rainforest. You take a clockwise circuit around the park, starting with a trek to its high point on the quieter, less-visited east side, followed by some fine viewpoints on the better-known south and west coast sides. Do exercise caution on the park's large rock outcroppings such as the summit and the rocky waterfront bluffs, as they can be quite slippery when wet.

From the north end of the Lions Gate Bridge, go west along Marine Drive in West Vancouver for not quite 10 kilometres (6 miles). Just past a fire hall on your right, go up a short rise in the road and turn left onto Beacon Lane, marked by a wooden Lighthouse Park sign. Follow Beacon Lane south to the parking lot.

Begin at the information kiosk at the top of the parking lot, where there is a large map of the park trails, as well as helpful hand-out maps. Walk past the yellow gate and turn left at the signposted Salal Loop Trail. This trail is somewhat rocky and rooty, and can be slippery when wet. Follow it uphill, staying to the right at the next three junctions. At the second fire hydrant, five to ten minutes from the start, turn right for a short scramble up a side trail leading you to the park's summit. Here you have a southerly viewpoint, albeit rather obstructed due to the surrounding trees.

Coming down from the summit, go right at the fire hydrant to continue east and downhill on the Summit Trail. This is a fairly rough trail, but easy to follow. Stay to the right at the next three junctions. About 10 minutes from the summit, you reach a sign-posted junction where the Arbutus Trail goes left, but you go right on the aptly named Valley of the Giants Trail. This trail is a

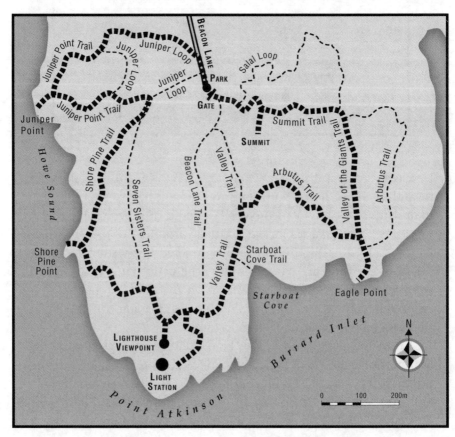

streambed during periods of heavy rainfall, but it does reward you with views of magnificent western red cedar, western hemlock and Douglas fir, some of which are over 60 metres (200 feet) tall and around 500 years old.

After another 10 minutes or so you reach another signposted junction with the Arbutus Trail. Continue straight ahead and out onto the rocky bluffs of Eagle Point. Here, amidst some hardy arbutus and pine, you are treated to 180-degree views of the North Shore, Lions Gate Bridge, Stanley Park, Vancouver and Point Grey.

Returning to the main trail again, go left on the Arbutus Trail, following it uphill then downhill, but generally west to its junction with the Valley Trail. If you are short of time you could turn right here to return directly to the parking lot.

Otherwise, go left to follow the Valley Trail south, then left again at the signposted junction for Starboat Cove. A comfortable bench on the bluff overlooking the water provides another fine southerly viewpoint. Return to the Valley Trail and continue west to the cluster of buildings at Point Atkinson, named in 1792 by Captain George Vancouver.

If the gate is open, you can walk down for a closer look at the lighthouse itself. The first lighthouse was built here in 1874. Seven

Looking northwest from Juniper Point.

years later the federal government spared the surrounding forest by reserving 75 hectares (185 acres) of land as a dark backdrop for the lighthouse beacon. You can also take in the interpretive centre at Phyl Munday House, open Sundays from 2:00 to 4:00 p.m. Volunteers maintain the centre, which is named in memory of Phyllis Munday (1894–1990), a renowned mountaineer, naturalist and Girl Guide leader.

From here you could return to the parking lot in 10 to 15 minutes by taking the Beacon Lane Trail north. Otherwise, continue west, following the "View" signs, to the nearby Lighthouse Viewpoint. Here you will find a historic cairn that names the past lighthouse keepers, and notes that the first white child born in West Vancouver, in 1876, was the son of the first keeper, Edwin Woodward.

Continuing northwest on the Shore Pine Trail, you pass a junction with Seven Sisters Trail and another signed lookout point before coming to Shore Pine Point (a.k.a. Jack Pine Point on the large wooden sign) about 10 to 15 minutes from the lighthouse. Here you have a fine view over to Bowen Island and the Coast Range off to the north.

Continue north on the Shore Pine Trail, staying left at its junction with Seven Sisters Trail. About 50 metres (165 feet) ahead, you could return to the parking lot in 5 minutes by taking the Juniper Loop Trail to the right. Otherwise, stay left at each of the Juniper Loop Trail junctions to follow the Juniper Point Trail down to the large rocky bluff of Juniper Point, about 20 minutes from Shore Pine Point.

To return, take the Juniper Point Trail left up the sturdy wooden staircase, and go left at a large rock face to reach its signposted junction with the Juniper Loop Trail. From here either way will take you out, but the left route is a little shorter, returning you to the parking lot 10 to 15 minutes from Juniper Point.

2 ▸ Whyte Lake

Elevation gain: 190 metres (620 feet)
High point: 320 metres (1,050 feet)
Season: Most of the year
Topographical map: North Vancouver 92G06
Hiking time: 2 to 2.5 hours
Dog-friendly

This quiet, interesting little trek follows the first few (easy) kilometres of the Knee Knackering North Shore Trail Run (KKNSTR) on your way to West Vancouver's rather secluded but very pretty Whyte Lake. It is also the recently improved access to the western end of the Baden-Powell (BP) trail (see hike #14), with the completion of the new Highway 1/99 Eagleridge Bypass in early 2009. The hike follows the Trans Canada Trail (TCT) through Nelson Canyon Park via Nelson Creek, then goes along Whyte Creek over to Whyte Lake, with an optional loop around part of the BP on the way back.

From Highway 1 in West Vancouver, you reach the trailhead by taking Exit 4, then turning left onto Westport Road. Go straight through at the four-way stop, follow Westport Road for about 1.5 kilometres (1 mile) and go under the highway before coming to a small gravel parking area on the right-hand side.

Begin by walking past the yellow gate, along the winding gravel road and back under the highway. In about five minutes you

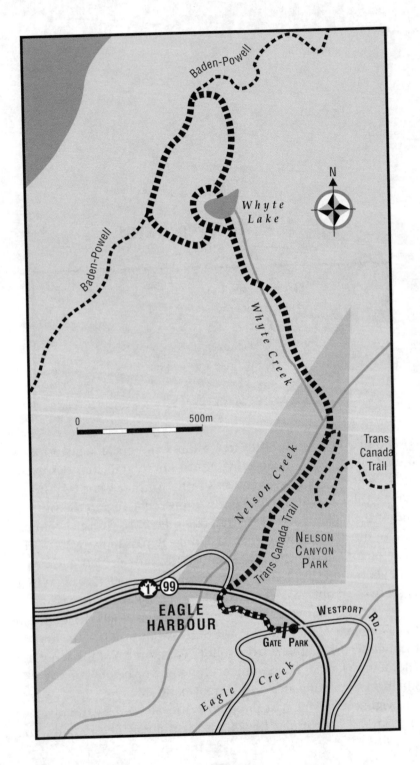

On the south shore of Whyte Lake.

come to a TCT sign, where you keep going straight ahead. After another couple of minutes turn right into the woods at a TCT (East) signpost. Following the winding uphill trail you soon hear Nelson Creek on your left. Nelson Creek was named after August Nelson, a local framer and planerman who had a mill site at Eagle Harbour in the 1890s.

About 15 to 20 minutes from the parking area, you leave the main trail by going down to your left at a marked junction with a large red cedar stump. In about 5 minutes this meandering trail leads to the Nelson Creek crossing on a sturdy footbridge built in 2008. This recently improved trail now heads west, following Whyte Creek on your left. Whyte Creek and Whyte Lake were named for Colonel Albert Whyte, an owner of the West Shore and Northern Land Company in the early 1900s. The company bought and developed land in the Horseshoe Bay and Whyte Cliff City area, the latter being renamed Whytecliff through the urging of Albert Whyte in 1914.

Shortly after taking a footbridge across Whyte Creek, and about 30 metres (100 feet) before reaching the first of three boardwalks across a marshy area, there is a short unmarked trail off to your right. This path leads to the south shore of Whyte Lake, just past the foundation of an old log cabin on your right. Back on the main trail, and after the third boardwalk, you come to a signposted junction. Access to the BP trail is to your left, but you follow the trail to your right, and in less than five minutes, watch for a small, unmarked trail that in another couple of minutes leads you down to Whyte Lake's serene northwest side. In the early 1900s a water flume was built to carry logs (from a commercial logging operation on Black Mountain) from here down to Horseshoe Bay.

From here you can retrace your steps back to the junction with the main Whyte Creek trail. However, if you have an extra 30 to 40 minutes and don't mind a little elevation gain, you can do a side trip out to the BP instead, by leaving the lakeside and turning right on the trail that brought you there. This trail is not well marked, but following coloured "BP" tapes on the trees, you take the trail roughly northwest up a fairly steep slope until it emerges at an unmarked junction with the BP in 15 to 20 minutes.

Turn left to go downhill on the BP, which is wide and rocky at this point. After another 10 to 15 minutes you reach an obvious but unmarked (other than by a large white Watershed warning sign on a tree) intersection with a trail branching off to the left. This is the trail back to Whyte Lake. You go up a fairly steep slope for a couple of minutes, then left and downhill to the junction where you originally turned off to get to the lake's shoreline.

To return to the parking area, start back along the boardwalk, noticing Eagle Bluff, the goal of the next few (not so easy) kilometres of the KKNSTR and the BP, looming up to the north at 1,094 metres (3,590 feet) elevation. You first follow Whyte Creek east, then Nelson Creek south, reaching your car about 40 to 50 minutes from the Whyte Lake junction.

3 ▸ Cypress Falls Park to Nelson Canyon Park

> **Elevation gain:** 250 metres (820 feet)
> **High point:** 440 metres (1,440 feet)
> **Season:** Most of the year
> **Topographical map:** North Vancouver 92G06
> **Hiking time:** 2 to 2.5 hours
> Dog-friendly

Here is a hike that introduces you to two of West Vancouver's lesser-known but quite charming parks: Cypress Falls Park, with its dramatic waterfalls; and Nelson Canyon Park, with its massive, second-growth Douglas firs and western red cedars. In between, a ramble along the Trans Canada Trail (TCT) makes this a satisfying outing almost any time of year. The hike starts in Cypress Falls Park and takes you along part of the TCT into Nelson Canyon Park. This is a one-way hike, so you may wish to leave a second car at the end to avoid a walk back along Westport Road.

From Highway 1 in West Vancouver you reach the trailhead by taking Exit 4, then turning right at the stop sign for Woodgreen Drive and right again at Woodgreen Place. Park in the upper parking area on your left just past the tennis courts.

To first leave a car at the other end, turn left from the Highway 1 exit onto Westport Road. Go straight through at the four-way stop and follow Westport Road for about 1.5 kilometres (1 mile) and go under the highway before coming to a small gravel parking area off to the right. Then follow Westport Road back to Woodgreen Drive and Woodgreen Place.

Begin by going straight east across the clearing into the forest. Turn left and head gradually uphill on the wide dirt trail. In a couple of minutes take the trail down to your right and follow it uphill, being wary of some steep drop-offs on your right-hand side. In about five minutes you come to the lower falls viewpoint.

Continue a little farther uphill until you reach a fence and warning sign, then make your way up to the left to return to the main trail. Go right and uphill for a few metres, then down to your right to a lookout over the waterfall. Follow this side trail up to a footbridge above the falls. Rather than cross the bridge, continue up the west side of Cypress Creek on the old, switch-backing dirt trail.

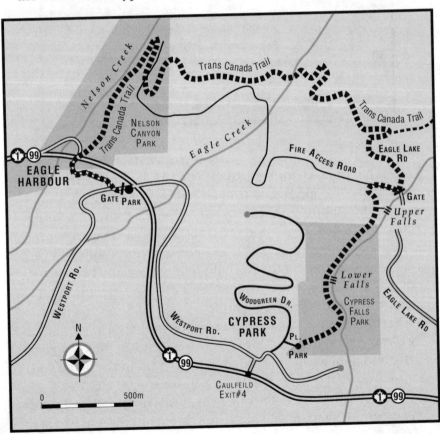

The lower falls in Cypress Falls Park.

This trail through some grand old Douglas firs is not well marked, but roughly parallels the creek on the way up and provides a view of a smaller waterfall on the way.

About 20 to 25 minutes from the start you reach a chain-link fence and gate with a British Pacific Properties sign. Go through the gate and continue uphill, still being wary of the steep drop-offs into the canyon, to the dramatic upper falls viewpoint about 5 minutes later. Then follow the trail up some large stone steps before it levels out and widens. About 5 minutes from the upper falls viewpoint you emerge onto a gravelled Fire Access Road. Turn right here and follow this road east and uphill for a couple of minutes to its junction with Eagle Lake Road.

The McCrady Bridge over Cypress Creek is on your right, but follow Eagle Lake Road left and uphill. About 10 minutes later you reach a TCT sign on your left. Turn left here and continue uphill for another few minutes to a TCT signposted junction. A right turn here would take you toward Cypress Bowl Road, but you go left, following the TCT west. Stay to the left at the next three "Watershed" sign junctions, following the TCT as it curves downhill and into the woods.

In another few minutes you cross the Eagle Creek footbridge, then continue through the forest of large, second-growth trees as the winding path makes its way roughly west and gradually downhill. Although the trail is not well marked, it is fairly easy to follow and there are occasional TCT signs on the trees.

About 20 to 25 minutes from Eagle Creek, you reach another TCT signposted junction. Going left on this service road would take you southeast back toward the Cypress Park area, but turn right and downhill into Nelson Canyon Park. Walk down some stairs and follow this pleasant trail south along the east side of Nelson Creek, which was named after August Nelson, a local framer and planer-man who had a mill site at Eagle Harbour in the 1890s. Just beyond the stairs you pass a large red cedar stump, where there is a marked junction with a connector trail heading west across Nelson Creek toward Whyte Lake (see hike #2) and the Baden-Powell trail (see hike #14), but you continue south down the TCT.

As the TCT emerges into a clearing a few minutes later, it goes to the right and west, but you stay left, following the winding gravel road downhill. At the next signposted junction, continue straight ahead to go under the highway (not to the right over a 1950s-era bridge). You then go past a yellow gate and out into a small parking area. If you had earlier left a car here, turn left onto Westport Road and follow it back to Woodgreen Drive and Woodgreen Place. Otherwise, the walk back is about half an hour.

4 ▸ Eagle Bluff and Black Mountain

> **Elevation gain:** 310 metres (1,015 feet)
> **High point:** 1,224 metres (4,015 feet)
> **Season:** July to October
> **Topographical map:** North Vancouver 92G06
> **Hiking time:** 4 to 5 hours, including lunch
> Dog-friendly

Spectacular, breathtaking vistas and a myriad of lovely little sub-alpine lakes await those who can manage the initial trek up the side of Black Mountain. The hike takes you from the Cypress Provincial Park Alpine (downhill) ski area up to Eagle Bluff and both Black Mountain summits, passing numerous lakes along the way. It is best done in mid-summer to early fall, long after the snow melts and before the fall rains start, as higher level sections of the trail can be muddy and slippery in places.

From Highway 1 in West Vancouver, you reach the trailhead by taking Exit 8 for Cypress Park, and following Cypress Bowl Road all the way up to the Alpine ski area pay parking lot.

Begin by following the "Baden-Powell (BP) Reroute to Black Mountain" signs from the trailhead signpost near the parking lot. Due to the 2010 Olympics construction, the former BP route to Black Mountain has been discontinued. The new, well-marked approach trail leads roughly northwest from the parking lot area, past the big lodge, around the base of the Black Chair and then west up the side of the ski area. You have a fairly steep, switch-backing uphill slog on this trail before coming out into the sub-alpine open area in 35 to 45 minutes. The very pretty Cabin Lake, a popular but cold swimming spot during the summer, is just a couple of minutes ahead along the boardwalk.

From the signposted Cabin Lake junction follow the BP dirt trail south into the woods. In about five minutes you reach the south summit of Black Mountain at 1,217 metres (3,993 feet), a large rock outcropping on your left with a 360-degree panoramic view. Continuing south on your way to Eagle Bluff, you next pass Owen Lake then the Cougar Lakes, both on your left. Shortly afterwards you come to Turtle Lake, with a large rock in the middle looking like a turtle shell, on your right. The trail through this area can be muddy in places before you descend into the woods on the last stretch to Eagle Bluff.

You will know when you have reached the 1,094-metre (3,590-foot) Eagle Bluff, about two kilometres and 45 minutes from Black Mountain. This viewpoint is absolutely spectacular, with

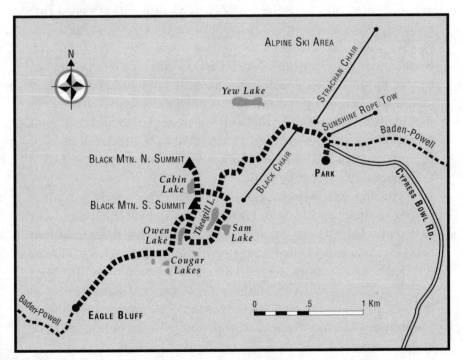

Looking southwest from the top of Eagle Bluff, with Bowen Island on the right.

magnificent views across the entire Lower Mainland, as well as east to Mount Baker and south to Point Roberts. Looking down and west you see Eagle Lake, Eagle Harbour, Horseshoe Bay, over to Bowen Island and up the Sunshine Coast. This is a good spot for lunch, but be sure to protect your meal from the quite bold whiskey jacks and ravens. Looking straight down from Eagle Bluff you get a feeling for the steep descent of the BP trail as it continues south and then west toward either the newer Nelson Canyon/Whyte Creek trailhead or the original Black Mountain trailhead near the Eagleridge Exit 2 from Highway 1 (see hike #14).

Retracing your steps back uphill and into the woods, you come to a signposted junction about 30 minutes from Eagle Bluff and just past Owen Lake. Go to the right here, following a short loop trail that takes you past Theagill Lake on your left and Sam Lake on your right. At the next signposted junction, go left to return to the Cabin Lake Trail. The trail to the right is no longer the return route to the parking lot due to the 2010 Olympics construction. In another few minutes you reach the next junction, where you can go right and downhill to the parking lot or left and back to the Cabin Lake junction in a couple of minutes.

From the Cabin Lake junction you can take one more side trip of about 250 metres (820 feet) north to 1,224-metre (4,015-foot) north summit of Black Mountain (a.k.a. Yew Lake Lookout). Here you are treated to views of the Lions, the Sea to Sky Highway and as far north as the Tantalus Range. Returning to the Cabin Lake junction, go left and head back downhill to the parking lot, watching your footing on the steep, switch-backing trail.

Hikers arriving at Eagle Bluff from the Black Mountain south summit.

5 ▸ St. Mark's Summit

Elevation gain: 435 metres (1,425 feet)
High point: 1,350 metres (4,430 feet)
Season: July to October
Topographical map: North Vancouver 92G06
Hiking time: 5 to 6 hours, including lunch
Dog-friendly

This hike is a short yet scenic introduction to the 29-kilometre (18-mile) high-level Howe Sound Crest Trail, providing great viewpoints of the Lions to the northeast and magnificent vistas over Howe Sound to the west. The trail continues on to Unnecessary Mountain, the Lions, Deeks Lake and Highway 99 just south of Porteau Cove for those backpackers desiring a much longer and more challenging outing. The hike starts in the Cypress Provincial Park Alpine (downhill) ski area and takes you 5.5 kilometres (3.4 miles) along the Howe Sound Crest Trail to St. Mark's Summit. It is best done in mid-summer to early fall, to avoid the snowy and muddy patches that linger well into summer at this elevation.

From Highway 1 in West Vancouver, you reach the trailhead by taking Exit 8 for Cypress Park, and following Cypress Bowl Road 14 kilometres (8.7 miles) up to the Alpine ski area pay parking lot.

There has been some rerouting of trails due to the 2010 Olympics construction, so begin by following the signs for the Howe Sound

Crest Trail from the trailhead signpost near the parking lot, staying to your right past the big lodge. About five minutes later you reach a signposted junction where the Yew Lake Trail continues straight ahead, but you turn right for the Howe Sound Crest Trail. There is a short ascent into the forest on this first section before you come out onto a gravel road. After a few minutes, you go right again at a signposted junction, following the somewhat rocky, rooty dirt trail into the woods before reaching another gravel road a few minutes later.

Continuing along briefly to the end of the road, you head into the woods again. This very pleasant trail along the lower western slopes of Mount Strachan is easy to follow and well marked with large, orange metal markers on the trees. About 30 minutes from the start you reach a signposted junction with a short side trail on your left to the Bowen Island Lookout. A few metres farther along the main trail a viewpoint to the Lions is on your right.

About 15 minutes later you emerge from the forest at Strachan

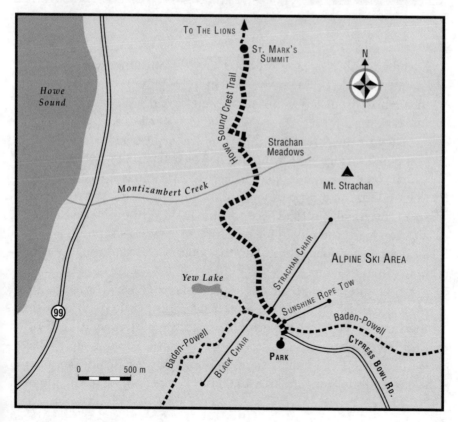

Highway 99, Horseshoe Bay and Bowen Island from St. Mark's Summit.

Meadows and cross Montizambert Creek. Notice the twin peaks of Mount Strachan up to your right. This is roughly the halfway point in the hike (in distance, not time), and a good spot for a break before tackling another 275 metres (900 feet) of elevation gain.

Back in the forest again, the trail now steepens somewhat as you climb a ridge, following a series of rocky, rooty switchbacks, which could be quite slippery when wet. The trail is still easy to follow, and for the most part you are sheltered from the sun by forest cover. Eventually, after a second similar ridge, the trail levels out and you reach the sub-alpine meadows of St. Mark's Summit, about an hour and a quarter from Montizambert Creek and roughly two hours from the start.

There are two spectacular viewpoints west over Howe Sound from the rocky knolls, one on each side of the little pond next to the trail. Be wary of going too close to the cliff edge at both of these viewpoints, as it is a very long way down. Looking out to the west you see Horseshoe Bay, Bowen Island, Bowyer Island, Gambier Island and the Sunshine Coast laid out before you. From the more northerly viewpoint you also look directly down at the vehicles on Highway 99.

Off to the north are views of Unnecessary Mountain and the Lions, possible objectives for a very long day's hike another time. For today, after taking in the superb views and enjoying your lunch, retrace your steps back to the parking lot.

Looking over to the Sunshine Coast from St. Mark's Summit.

6 ► Hollyburn Peak

Elevation gain: 435 metres (1,425 feet)
High point: 1,325 metres (4,350 feet)
Season: July to October
Topographical map: North Vancouver 92G06
Hiking time: 3 to 4 hours
Dog-friendly

Hollyburn Peak was first climbed in 1908 and is a most rewarding objective with its panoramic mountain views. Today climbing
Hollyburn need only be a relatively short, half-day outing, a far cry
from the 1920s when hikers would make the trek up old logging
trails from the West Vancouver ferry terminus at Ambleside. This
hike is also quite suitable for the family, with children frequently
seen accompanying their parents on the trail, but allow a little extra
time. The hike takes you from the Cypress Provincial Park Nordic
(cross-country) ski area along part of the Baden-Powell (BP) trail,
then up the Hollyburn Mountain Trail to Hollyburn Peak. A short
side trip on the way back can take you past First Lake and the historic Hollyburn Lodge. This hike is best done in mid-summer or
early fall, long after the snow melts and before the fall rains start, as
the Hollyburn Mountain Trail can be muddy and slippery in places.

From Highway 1 in West Vancouver, you reach the trailhead
by taking Exit 8 for Cypress Park, and following Cypress Bowl Road

about 13 kilometres (8 miles) up to the Nordic ski area pay parking lot.

Begin by taking the gravel path uphill from the trailhead kiosk, and going to your left near the woods to follow the Powerline Road north. (Going to your right along the power lines would take you to Hollyburn Lodge and First Lake; see hike #8, or take the optional side trip on your return as described below.) Looking over to your left on the way up the trail, you see Black Mountain with its

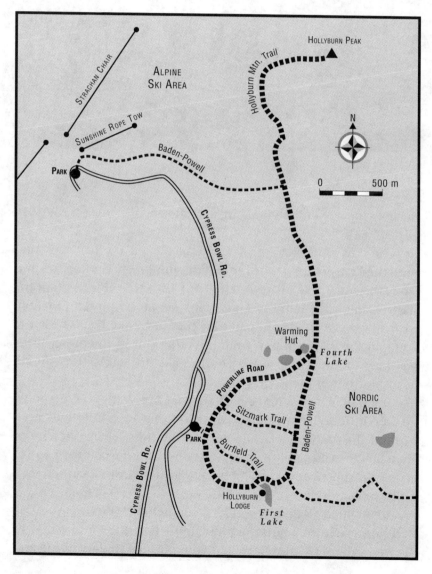

Hikers on top of Hollyburn Peak.

newly sculptured freestyle skiing and snowboard runs for the 2010 Olympics.

The Powerline Road rises fairly steeply for the first few minutes, then crosses under the power lines just before coming to Third Lake, the small lake on your left about 10 to 15 minutes from the start. A couple of minutes later you reach a signposted junction, with a large, green warming hut on your left. Here you turn left as you join the BP coming in from the other side of the power lines. Just past the warming hut is Fourth Lake on your left as the BP heads north into the woods.

The trail, which alternates in and out of forest cover as you go up, is a little rough and rocky in places, but easy to follow, even without the orange metal markers on the trees. Blueberries are in abundance on Hollyburn in late summer and it's common to see people picking near the trail, but be aware that bears are often seen eating here as well.

About 40 to 50 minutes and 2.2 kilometres (1.4 miles) from the start you reach the signposted junction where the BP turns off to the west toward Cypress Bowl, but you continue straight ahead and a little more steeply uphill for another 1.9 kilometres (1.2 miles) toward Hollyburn Peak. (The Alpine ski area at Cypress Bowl is a possible alternative starting point for this hike, with approximately the same time and distance to reach this point; see hike #15 for the trail description.)

About 20 minutes or so from the BP junction a short side trail to your right leads to a bench and lookout point east toward Crown, Goat and Grouse mountains. A few minutes later you reach a very pretty open area, the Heather Lakes, with its rocky outcroppings and picturesque little ponds.

Another 10 to 15 minutes, with a little scramble up a rocky section at the end, finds you at Hollyburn Peak, with its spectacular vistas in all directions. Landmarks include the twin peaks of Mount Strachan to the northwest and the Lions to the north, with the snow-capped peaks of the Coast Range beyond. Crown, Grouse and Goat mountains are off to the east, with Cathedral Mountain looming beyond.

There are lots of spots for a lunch or snack break other than the rocky peak itself, but be sure to guard your food from the quite aggressive whiskey jacks and ravens. After a well-deserved break, retrace your steps back down to the warming hut at the power lines.

From here you could continue downhill and back to the parking lot. Otherwise, if you have an extra half hour or so, follow the BP straight across the clearing under the power lines and into the woods. Here you begin heading downhill on Upper Wells Gray, one of the major cross-country ski trails. In about 15 minutes you reach a signposted turnoff on your right for a short connector trail to Hollyburn Lodge, originally opened as Hollyburn Ski Camp in early 1927, and the very pretty First Lake, the site of an impressive ski jump in those early days. When you have explored enough here, follow the signs from behind the lodge back west to the parking lot in about 10 minutes.

7 ▸ Hollyburn Cabin Country

> **Elevation gain:** 190 metres (620 feet)
> **High point:** 950 metres (3,115 feet)
> **Season:** July to October
> **Topographical map:** North Vancouver 92G06
> **Hiking time:** 2.5 to 3 hours
> Dog-friendly

Since the 1920s, generations of Hollyburn hikers and skiers have developed an intricate network of trails and built cabins of every description as bases for their weekend getaways and wilderness adventures. This rewarding trek introduces you to part of that Hollyburn Ridge trail system and some of the eclectic old cabins that remain. The hike takes you on a loop up the old West Lake Road, along part of the Baden-Powell (BP) trail to First Lake and Hollyburn Lodge, then down the old Forks Trail back to the start. It is best done in mid-summer to early fall, after the snow melts and before the fall rains start, as higher level sections of these trails can be muddy and slippery in places.

From Highway 1 in West Vancouver you reach the trailhead by taking Exit 8 for Cypress Park and following Cypress Bowl Road up for about 11 kilometres (7 miles), passing first Highview Lookout and then Quarry Lookout. Just past the next hairpin turn there is a gravel parking area on the right-hand side for access to West Lake Road.

Begin by following this wide, gravel service road uphill, staying right at two junctions with other gravel roads. In 10 minutes or so you pass a yellow gate blocking further vehicle access to the area, then cross a bridge over Marr Creek. Stay right at the next trail junction, and about 10 minutes past Marr Creek you reach an unmarked junction with a small trail on your right. This trail, actually the most northerly piece of the Old Brewis Trail (see hike #10), leads gradually downhill and is fairly easy to follow, with occasional red markers on the trees. In just a few minutes you come to a decrepit old log cabin, minus its roof, about 20 metres (65 feet) over to your left. It looks old enough to be one of the originals from the early 1900s. Just ahead the trail descends to a steep and challenging crossing of the east branch of McDonald Creek, so you retrace your steps back uphill to the West Lake Road trail.

Continue uphill on this rough, rocky road, staying left at the next two forks in the road. About 15 minutes from the Brewis Trail

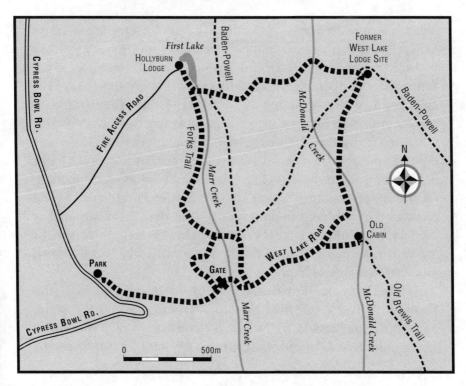

Picnickers at First Lake, with Hollyburn Lodge to the left.

side trip you reach a large, open area, the site of the former Westlake Ski Lodge, which was originally moved piecemeal from West Lake in 1938 but which burned to the ground over 20 years ago. Go left at the BP trail signpost just ahead and continue uphill toward the cross-country ski area, saving the access trail to Blue Gentian Lake, a few metres ahead on your right, for another day (see hike #8).

Turn right at the next BP signpost a couple of minutes later to go up a narrow, rocky trail with views east to Indian Arm and Mount Baker on a good day. Go right at the next BP signposted junction, where the BP becomes a wide, cross-country ski trail (the Grand National). As you continue up, stay left on the Grand National at the Jack Pratt junction. Next you pass an access trail on your right for West Lake (again a good outing for another day; see hike #8), followed by a couple of private cabins.

At the next signposted junction, 20 to 25 minutes from the Westlake Ski Lodge site, the BP continues north, but you follow the sign left for the Burfield Trail to reach First Lake. Once you've had a look around First Lake and Hollyburn Lodge, return to the Nasmyth

Bridge over Marr Creek at the south end of the lake and locate the sign for the Forks Trail, next to a large trail map.

Follow the Forks Trail downhill, with Marr Creek on your left, noting the numerous private cabins secluded in the woods on either side. About 10 minutes later, stay left at the "Trail" sign junction, following this very pleasant, winding trail gradually downhill through more cabin country. About 15 to 20 minutes from the start, the trail becomes a recently upgraded fine gravel path. One branch leads left to more cabins on the other side of a well-built footbridge over Marr Creek and the other continues downhill.

Staying to the right and continuing downhill, you reach a large gravel parking area a couple of minutes later. Go right here and follow the gravel road downhill. About five minutes later you reach its junction with West Lake Road, where you go right again and retrace your steps back out to Cypress Bowl Road and your car.

Otherwise, going left and crossing the bridge provides an alternate return route. There is an old picnic table and bench on your right a couple of minutes across the bridge. In the brush nearby are concrete footings from the terminus of the old Hollyburn chairlift, built in 1950 but destroyed in a fire in 1965. This is also the site of the former Hi-View Lodge, built in the early 1950s but burned down in the same fire.

At the four-way trail junction another couple of minutes on, there are three options. If you have time for some more exploring, the gravel road on your left takes you past a few cabins and back up to First Lake in 15 to 20 minutes. Continuing on the trail straight ahead takes you past some more cabins and back to the Westlake Ski Lodge site in the same amount of time. Otherwise, go down to your right to reach West Lake Road in less than 5 minutes. Turn right here and retrace your steps back across Marr Creek, past the yellow gate and out to Cypress Bowl Road in about 10 minutes.

8 ▸ Hollyburn Lakes Circuit

> **Elevation gain:** 220 metres (720 feet)
> **High point:** 950 metres (3,115 feet)
> **Season:** July to October
> **Topographical map:** North Vancouver 92G06
> **Hiking time:** 3 to 3.5 hours
> Dog-friendly

Hollyburn Ridge is blessed with numerous pretty little sub-alpine lakes to attract the hiker. This rewarding circuit of its trail system treats you to four of these in one outing, with only moderate elevation gain along the way. You go through the Cypress Provincial Park Nordic (cross-country) ski area to Hollyburn Lodge and First Lake, then around to West Lake, Lost Lake and Blue Gentian Lake before heading back. This hike is best done in mid-summer to early fall, long after the snow melts and before the fall rains start, as some of these trails can be muddy and slippery in places.

From Highway 1 in West Vancouver, you reach the trailhead by taking Exit 8 for Cypress Park, and following Cypress Bowl Road about 13 kilometres (8 miles) up to the Nordic ski area pay parking lot.

Begin by following the gravel path uphill from the trailhead kiosk, staying to your right near the woods (going left along the power lines leads up toward Hollyburn Peak; see hike #6), and taking the trail east under the "Hollyburn Trail to Hollyburn Lodge" sign. In about 10 minutes you reach the red Hollyburn Lodge, originally opened as Hollyburn Ski Camp in early 1927, and First Lake, the site of an impressive ski jump in those early days. There are some benches and picnic tables near the lake. Go past the Ranger Station, crossing the Nasmyth Bridge over Marr Creek at the south end of the lake, and up the dirt road on the other side to the signpost-ed Baden-Powell (BP) trail junction. Turn right and follow the BP downhill for about 5 minutes to the West Lake Trail signpost.

Go left here to follow this wide dirt trail for about 10 minutes to West Lake. This spot was the site of the original West Lake Lodge, which was opened in 1933 but closed and dismantled in 1938 when West Vancouver wanted to include the area in the Brother's Creek watershed. Part of the structure of a ski jump built in 1934 can still be seen in the water at the north end of the lake.

From West Lake, take the signposted 440-metre (1,440-foot) trail for Blue Gentian Lake, following Stoney Creek south and downhill. The trail is quite easy to follow, but is fairly rough and can be muddy in places. At the next signposted junction, go left for the Lost Lake/Blue Gentian Lake trail. In about another 5 minutes you see

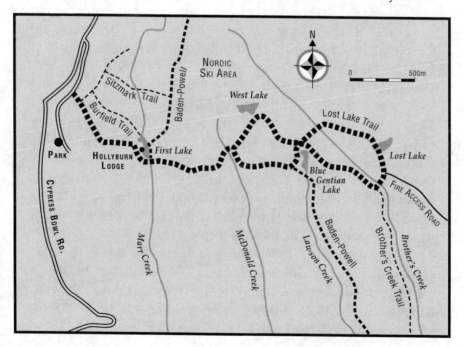

West Lake, near the site of the original 1930s West Lake Lodge.

Blue Gentian Lake on your right, but save that detour for the way back and take the Lost Lake Trail to the left. This trail is rougher and not as well marked as the others. It crosses first Stoney Creek and then Brother's Creek, taking you to Lost Lake (originally known as East Lake) in another 25 to 35 minutes.

Leaving Lost Lake, take the trail on the right-hand side, heading south and downhill. In about 400 metres (1,315 feet) and another 10 to 15 minutes you come to Brother's Creek again. The trail down to your left is the Fire Access Road heading south, but you take the footbridge across the creek then go to your right, up the Brother's Creek Trail toward Blue Gentian Lake. This pleasant trail has markers on the trees and is quite easy to follow. In 20 to 30 minutes you reach Blue Gentian Lake (known as Middle Lake back in the 1920s), where you can rest at the lakeside picnic table.

Next, follow the boardwalk around to the west side of the lake, passing the trail junction for the other lakes on your right. If you are there in late summer, watch for the lake's namesake king gentian flowers near the boardwalk before heading into the woods on the 300-metre (985-foot) trail to the BP junction.

Go right here to follow the BP uphill. In about five minutes you come to a large clearing, the second site of the West Lake Lodge, which was moved piecemeal from West Lake and reconstructed here in 1938 as the Westlake Ski Lodge. It was later renamed Cypress Park Resort, but after almost 50 years of operation it burned to the ground in 1986.

Go right at the signposted junction to continue uphill on the wide, rocky BP. At the next clearing, in about five more minutes, follow the BP to the right into the woods and up a narrow, rocky trail with views east to Indian Arm and Mount Baker. At the next signposted junction, in another five minutes, go right as the BP becomes a wide, cross-country ski trail (the Grand National). As you continue up, stay left on the Grand National at the Jack Pratt junction. On your way up you pass a couple of private cabins, as well as the turnoff you took earlier for West Lake.

About 20 to 25 minutes from the West Lake Lodge site you reach another signposted junction. Here the BP continues north, but you follow the sign left for the Burfield Trail, retracing your steps to First Lake, Hollyburn Lodge and then the parking lot.

9 ▶ Trans Canada Trail/ Millstream Trail Loop

Elevation gain: 290 metres (950 feet)
High point: 670 metres (2,200 feet)
Season: May to November
Topographical map: North Vancouver 92G06
Hiking time: 2.5 to 3 hours
Dog-friendly

This ambitious but rewarding trek on the slopes of lower Hollyburn treats you to a variety of terrain and crossings of several major West Vancouver creeks. It also passes Highview Lookout on Cypress Bowl Road and includes a visit to the Shields Log Dam and Flume Pond from the early 1900s. The hike follows part of the Lawson Creek Forestry Heritage Walk (named for John Lawson, one of West Vancouver's leading pioneers, and responsible for several major community achievements during the early 1900s), as it takes you from the lower Millstream Road trailhead, up the Brewis Trail, then west along the Trans Canada Trail (TCT) to the Forks Trail for a loop back along the Millstream Trail.

From Highway 1 in West Vancouver you reach the trailhead by taking Exit 11, going north on Crosscreek Road, then left onto Chartwell Drive, following Chartwell up to its intersection with

Eyremount Drive and Millstream Road, where there is a yellow gate marking the trailhead.

Begin by going west from the gate along the dirt road for about 10 minutes, passing a signposted junction with a Fire Access Road and then crossing Lawson Creek before coming to the Brewis Trail junction on your right. This trail is not well marked, but easy to follow. You climb steadily uphill for 20 to 30 minutes before coming to the TCT/Skyline Trail at the power lines, where you go left.

Watch for the occasional yellow TCT signs on the trees, and follow this very pleasant trail west as it moves alternately from forest cover to open stretches under the power lines. It crosses several creeks along the way, with deep ravines for the three different branches of McDonald Creek and then Marr Creek. After 40 to 50 minutes from the Brewis Trail junction, you reach the TCT/Skyline Trail's junction with the Forks Trail, marked by a TCT signpost.

The TCT/Skyline Trail continues west, while the branch of the Forks Trail a few metres ahead on your right heads north, leading up toward West Lake Road, Hollyburn cabin country and Hollyburn Lodge (see hike #7). You go down to the left, following the Forks Trail in a generally southeasterly direction. It is rough and not well marked, but fairly well worn and easy to follow. After 25 to

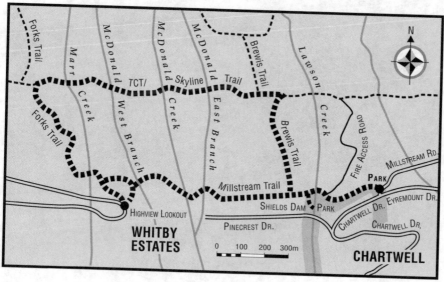

30 minutes of downhill travel, you cross Marr Creek again, and in about another 5 minutes you come to an unmarked (other than by a large British Pacific Properties sign on a tree) junction with the Millstream Trail heading east.

You can see Highview Lookout on the Cypress Bowl Road through the trees, and may want to take a slight detour to the right to check out this spectacular view. Otherwise, take the Millstream Trail to your left (east), bearing slightly uphill before descending to the first footbridge. In 10 to 15 minutes, after crossing all three branches of McDonald Creek again, the trail widens out to look more like the old logging road that it is. Continue following it east for 25 to 30 minutes from the lookout to a chain-link fence and gate next to a signposted junction with a trail leading down to Pinecrest Drive.

Before returning to Millstream Road, if time permits, go down this winding trail for a couple of minutes to the Shields Dam Park. The park is the site of the Shields Log Dam and Flume Pond, built in 1917 and used until 1926. It was used to store floating cedar shingle bolts (long, wedge-shaped blocks of cedar from which shakes and shingles were cut), and to supply water to the wooden flume that

Outlet of the 1920s' Shields Log Dam and Flume Pond.

transported the shingle bolts to the shingle mill two kilometres below. To return to your car, go back up to the Millstream Trail junction, turn right, cross the Lawson Creek footbridge and retrace your steps out to the Millstream Road gate.

A double footbridge over Lawson Creek on the Millstream Trail.

10 ▸ The Old Brewis Trail

Elevation gain: 280 metres (920 feet)
High point: 660 metres (2,165 feet)
Season: May to November
Topographical map: North Vancouver 92G06
Hiking time: 2 to 2.5 hours
Dog-friendly

Here is another energetic outing that closely follows the Lawson Creek Forestry Heritage Walk and passes historical remnants of early 1900s' logging activities as well as the massive, 1,100-year-old Hollyburn Fir. The hike takes you from the lower Millstream Road trailhead, part way up Brother's Creek, then along the Crossover Trail to the Old Brewis Trail for a loop back to the start. The Brewis name has long been associated with the Hollyburn area, with R.D. Brewis being the builder of the original West Lake Lodge in the winter of 1932–33.

From Highway 1 in West Vancouver, you reach the trailhead by taking Exit 11, going north on Crosscreek Road, then left onto Chartwell Drive, following Chartwell up to its intersection with Eyremount Drive and Millstream Road, where there is a yellow gate marking the trailhead.

Begin by going west along the dirt road for about 5 minutes until you reach a signposted junction with the Fire Access Road leading north. Turn right and follow this road uphill, passing through a chain-link gate before you come to a signposted junction for the Shields Incline Railway. The railway was part of an old cable system built in the early 1920s to transport cedar shingle bolts (long, wedge-shaped blocks of cedar from which shakes and shingles were cut) down the mountainside to the Shields Log Dam and Flume Pond, but abandoned in 1926. Turn right, following this trail uphill

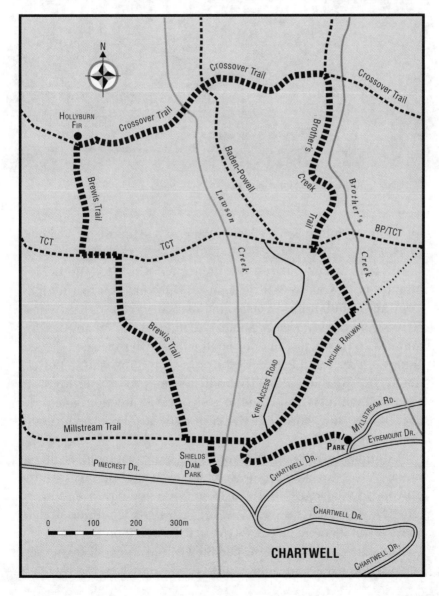

The giant 1,100-year-old Hollyburn Fir.

for about 10 minutes, when you come to a signpost for Brother's Creek.

Go left here, up the west side of Brother's Creek for another few minutes until you come to a signpost directing you to the right. Continue uphill, noting a large granite rock on your right, a glacial erratic from the last ice age about 12,000 years ago. In another few minutes you come to a signposted junction with the Baden-Powell/ Trans Canada Trail (BP/TCT) at the power lines. Turn left, following the BP/TCT past an old BC Hydro helicopter pad on your right. In about five minutes you come to a signposted junction where the BP/TCT continues west, but you turn right to follow the Brother's Creek trail north.

Continue steadily uphill through the more mature forest alongside Brother's Creek, being wary of some steep drop-offs into the canyon on your right. In 10 to 15 minutes you pass a signposted junction with the Crossover Trail on your right. Continue straight ahead about 25 more metres (80 feet), then go left on the Crossover Trail, heading west toward the Old Brewis Trail. The trail crosses several old skid roads and is difficult to follow in places, but there are occasional red metal markers on the trees. You cross the BP again in 15 to 20 minutes and then Lawson Creek a few metres farther on.

After another 10 minutes or so you reach the signposted site of the giant Hollyburn Fir on your right. This living Douglas fir, about three metres (ten feet) in diameter and thought to be almost 1,100 years old, was spared during the early 1900s logging because the loggers were mainly interested in the western red cedar. It was rediscovered in 1985 during the Big Tree Registry project of the Ministry of Forests.

Just past the Hollyburn Fir you reach the Crossover Trail's junction with the Old Brewis Trail. To the right the Brewis leads up to a steep and challenging crossing of McDonald Creek's east branch, then beyond that to West Lake Road, from which you can reach Hollyburn cabin country and Hollyburn Lodge (see hike #7). But you go left, following the red markers on the trees to take the Brewis downhill for about 15 minutes to the TCT/Skyline Trail at the power lines.

Go left along this trail for about 150 metres (500 feet) until you reach the signposted junction with the Lower Brewis trail. This trail is not well marked, but easy to follow. After 15 minutes or so of downhill you reach the Millstream Trail junction. Turn left here, following the trail east for a couple of minutes to a chain-link fence and gate next to a signposted junction with a trail leading down to Pinecrest Drive.

Before returning to Millstream Road, if time permits, go down this winding trail for a couple of minutes to the Shields Dam Park. This is the site of the Shields Log Dam and Flume Pond, built in 1917 and used until 1926. It was used to store floating cedar shingle bolts, and to supply water to the wooden flume that transported the shingle bolts to the shingle mill two kilometres (one mile) below. To return to your car, go back up to the Millstream Trail junction, turn right, cross the Lawson Creek footbridge and retrace your steps out to the Millstream Road gate.

11 ▸ Upper Brother's Creek

> **Elevation gain:** 340 metres (1,115 feet)
> **High point:** 720 metres (2,360 feet)
> **Season:** May to November
> **Topographical map:** North Vancouver 92G06
> **Hiking time:** 2 to 2.5 hours
> Dog-friendly

On this hike along part of the Brother's Creek Forestry Heritage Walk, you enjoy breathtaking views of the Brother's Creek upper canyon and waterfalls and pass by some magnificent examples of old-growth cedar and fir on the way back. Starting from the upper Millstream Road trailhead, you go along the Crossover Trail to the upper part of Brother's Creek, then circle back to Millstream via the Brother's Creek Fire Access Road.

From Highway 1 in West Vancouver you reach the trailhead by taking Exit 11, going north on Crosscreek Road, left onto Chartwell Drive, then onto Millstream Road, staying left on Millstream to park just past Henlow Road.

Begin by going through the Fire Road gate and following the wide, rocky trail (formerly the path of the Walking Dudley, a steam locomotive used by the McNair-Fraser Lumber Company to transport logs down the steep slopes from 1908 to 1913) for about 5 minutes to a signposted junction with the Baden-Powell/Trans Canada

Trail (BP/TCT) at Hadden Creek. Turn left here and then right at the power lines junction to follow the Brother's Creek Fire Access Road into the woods. In another 10 to 15 minutes you reach a signposted junction with the Crossover Trail on your left. Follow this trail west toward Brother's Creek.

In a few minutes you reach an obvious but unmarked junction with a long, straight trail angled roughly northeast-southwest down the hill. This is the Shields Incline Railway, part of an old cable railway built in the early 1920s to transport cedar shingle bolts (long, wedge-shaped blocks of cedar from which shakes and shingles were

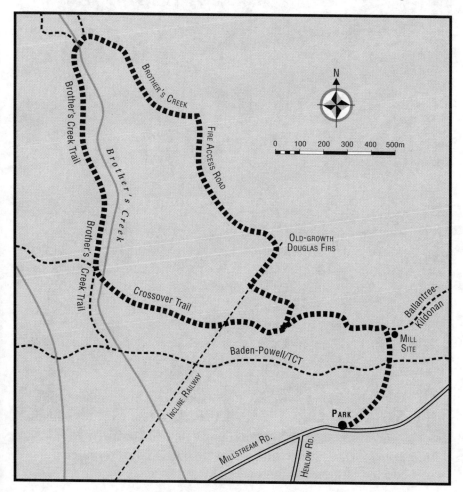

Shelf-like bracket fungi and an old sign pointing the way to Lost Lake decorate a large Douglas fir at the upper Brother's Creek footbridge.

cut) down to a shingle mill several kilometres below, but abandoned in 1926. Cross the old railway bed and continue straight ahead up the hill on the Crossover Trail, following the occasional orange markers on the trees.

Soon you begin to hear Brother's Creek on your left and in 15 to 20 minutes from the Incline Railway you reach the footbridge to the other side. Cross the bridge and turn up to your right. In about 25 metres (80 feet) the Crossover Trail continues west toward the BP and Brewis trails (see hike #10), but you stay right, taking the Brother's Creek Trail north. Continue following this very pleasant trail gradually uphill, but be wary of some steep drop-offs into the canyon on your right. Watch for an impressive double waterfall about 20 minutes from the Crossover Trail junction. A short but steep side trail can lead you to a small beach area under the falls, if the water level is low enough. Some 5 minutes past the waterfall you reach another footbridge across Brother's Creek.

Cross here, leaving the trails to Blue Gentian Lake and Lost Lake (on the east side of the bridge) for another day (see hike #8), and take the wide, rocky Fire Access Road downhill to your right. On the way down watch for some of the magnificent old-growth western red cedar and Douglas fir trees that are still standing.

About 25 to 30 minutes from the footbridge you come to a switchback where the trail turns sharply to the right. Here you see a small signpost (numbered #5 & #6) on your left. A short trail with small red markers on the trees leads straight ahead into the forest. In about 7 minutes you reach the pitchfork-like Candelabra tree, a dead, old-growth Douglas fir about 60 metres (200 feet) in height and 3 metres (10 feet) in diameter. Follow the red markers downhill another 3 minutes or so to a tall, living old-growth Douglas fir of a similar diameter.

Retrace your steps back up to the Fire Access Road and continue to follow it downhill. After about 20 minutes, at its junction with the Ballantree–Kildonan Trail (see hike #12) on your left, check out what remains of an old mill boiler house and steam sawmill site, built in 1912 but abandoned in 1913. Then continue downhill, reaching the junction with the BP/TCT trail at the power lines in another few minutes. Go down to your left, where in a couple of minutes you reach the Hadden Creek junction again. Take the trail down to the right and back out to Millstream Road.

12 ▸ Brother's Creek/Ballantree Park

> **Elevation gain:** 240 metres (790 feet)
> **High point:** 620 metres (2,040 feet)
> **Season:** May to November
> **Topographical map:** North Vancouver 92G06
> **Hiking time:** 2.5 to 3.5 hours
> Dog-friendly

Here is a challenging yet rewarding circuit, with canyon and waterfall views, a lovely trek through a little-known forested West Vancouver park and a visit to relics of early 1900s' logging activity along the way. This hike, which follows part of the Brother's Creek Forestry Heritage Walk, takes you from the lower Millstream Road trailhead, part way up Brother's Creek, over to Ballantree Park via the Crossover Trail, then back to Millstream via the Baden-Powell/Trans Canada Trail (BP/TCT).

From Highway 1 in West Vancouver you reach the trailhead by taking Exit 11, going north on Crosscreek Road, then left onto Chartwell Drive, following Chartwell up to its intersection with Eyremount Drive and Millstream Road, where there is a yellow gate marking the trailhead.

Begin by going west along the dirt road for about 5 minutes until you reach a signposted junction with the Fire Access Road heading north. Turn right and follow this road uphill, passing a chain-link gate and then a signposted junction for the Shields Incline Railway.

This railway was part of an old cable system built in the early 1920s to transport cedar shingle bolts (long, wedge-shaped blocks of cedar from which shakes and shingles were cut) down the mountainside to the Shields Log Dam and Flume Pond, but abandoned in 1926. It will be part of your return route. Continue uphill on the winding dirt road until after 25 to 30 minutes from the start you reach a signposted junction with the BP/TCT. Turn right, following this trail under the power lines and into the woods again, heading east on the BP/TCT. Go left at its signposted junction with the Brother's Creek Trail a few minutes later.

Continue steadily uphill alongside Brother's Creek, being wary of some steep drop-offs into the canyon on your right. After another 10 to 15 minutes you come to a footbridge across Brother's Creek. Cross here and follow the Crossover Trail southeast and downhill. In about 15 minutes, just after a small footbridge, you reach an obvious but unmarked junction with a long, straight trail angled roughly northeast-southwest down the hill. This is another section of the Incline Railway you passed earlier. Continue downhill on the Crossover Trail for another 5 minutes or so, when you reach its

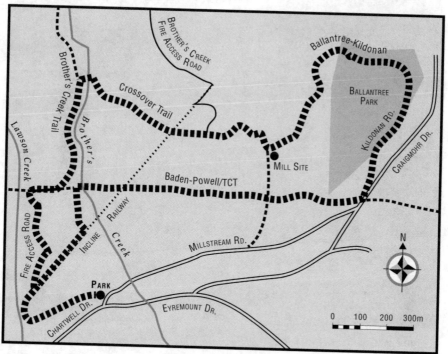

The Brother's Creek lower falls in spring runoff.

signposted junction with the Brother's Creek Fire Access Road. Turn right to follow this road downhill. In about 10 minutes you reach its signposted junction with the Ballantree–Kildonan trail. Before going left here, check out the remains of the old mill boiler house and steam sawmill site mentioned in hike #11.

The Ballantree–Kildonan trail is a fairly old, easy to follow, pleasing trail, albeit with only occasional red markers on the trees. It makes its way uphill in a generally northeasterly direction, then curves gradually southeasterly and downhill. After about a half hour from the Fire Access Road you reach a Ballantree Trail signpost. Go down to the right here, across a footbridge, then to the left and over a second footbridge. Stay to your right through an open area in about 5 minutes, then continue straight ahead and roughly south on the winding dirt path. About 10 minutes from the Ballantree Trail signpost you emerge at the top of Kildonan Road.

Follow Kildonan down to Craigmohr Drive, continuing down to the Millstream Road/Craigmohr intersection a couple of minutes later. On your right is a BP/TCT signpost, where you go up the stairs and follow the trail into the forest, paralleling the power lines on your left-hand side. About 10 minutes later you reach the Hadden Creek signposted junction, where you stay to the right, taking a gravel road back uphill. Stay left at the Fire Access Road junction to follow the BP/TCT west, back under the power lines and into the woods as it gradually gains some elevation.

In about 20 minutes you pass another signposted junction with the Incline Railway. In another few minutes you begin to hear Brother's Creek and you pass a lookout spot with views of Stanley Park, downtown Vancouver and beyond. Descend to a footbridge for the Brother's Creek crossing, with its very impressive waterfall during spring runoff. Just after climbing up from the Brother's Creek canyon, go left and downhill at a BP/TCT signposted junction onto a lower section of the Brother's Creek Trail.

In about 10 minutes you come to its unmarked junction with the Incline Railway, where you turn right to follow this old railway bed southwest and downhill. In another 10 minutes or so you reach its junction with the Fire Access Road. From here you go left and retrace your steps back down to the Millstream Trail then left and out to Millstream Road.

13 ▸ Ballantree Park from Cleveland Dam

> **Elevation gain:** 330 metres (1,080 feet)
> **High point:** 480 metres (1,575 feet)
> **Season:** April to November
> **Topographical map:** North Vancouver 92G06
> **Hiking time:** 2.5 to 3 hours
> Dog-friendly

Here is a hike that truly offers some variety, with stunning views from Cleveland Dam in North Vancouver to the secluded forests of Ballantree Park in West Vancouver. You follow the Baden-Powell (BP) Trail from Cleveland Dam up into West Vancouver, take the Ballantree–Kildonan trail around Ballantree Park, then return to Cleveland Dam.

You can shorten the hiking time by 45 minutes or so by leaving a second car at the upper Millstream Road trailhead in West Vancouver. That trailhead is reached by taking Exit 11 on Highway 1, going north on Crosscreek Road, left onto Chartwell Drive, then onto Millstream, and staying left on Millstream to park just after passing Henlow Road.

From Highway 1 in North Vancouver take Exit 14 to go north on Capilano Road. Follow it up to the paved parking lot on your left, just past Clements Avenue but before Nancy Greene Way heads up toward Grouse Mountain.

Begin by walking across Cleveland Dam, admiring the views of Capilano Lake, the Lions and Grouse Mountain up on your right, then the awe-inspiring spillway and vertical canyon walls to your left. This dam was completed in 1954 and named after Ernest A. Cleveland, the first chief commissioner of the Greater Vancouver Water District from 1926 to 1952. Across the dam you see two gravel roads on your left. The lower one leads into Capilano Canyon, a good destination for another day (see hike #18), but you take the upper one with the BP signplate.

The BP is well marked with orange "BP" fleur-de-lis triangles on the trees. Follow it uphill, passing the Shinglebolt Trail junction on your left. After about 10 minutes, just before coming to a chain-link fence at the end of the road, you turn left into the woods at a BP signpost. The trail begins with a fairly steep but short uphill, followed by a brief downhill before emerging onto Glenmore Drive in another 15 minutes or so. Pick up the trail directly across Glenmore Drive, following it west as it begins a gradual ascent through the residential areas of the British Properties. You continue uphill, following the power lines, crossing three more streets and noting the TCT (Trans Canada Trail) and BP markers as you go.

After 40 to 60 minutes of steady climbing on the BP/TCT from Glenmore Drive, you come to a green metal gate and a Millstream

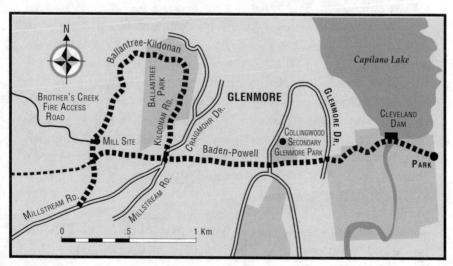

Old mill boiler house and steam sawmill site from 1912–13.

Road/Craigmohr Drive street sign. Turn right here up Craigmohr, then after a couple of minutes go left onto Kildonan Road. In about another 5 minutes you reach the Ballantree Park trailhead at the top of Kildonan.

Follow the trail roughly north into the woods, keeping to the left when you reach an open area in about 5 minutes. In another 5 minutes or so you see a footbridge over a small creek on your left. Cross the creek, then go right and cross a second footbridge. In a couple of minutes you come to a mossy old bench and the Ballantree Trail signpost, informing you that you will reach the Fire Access Road junction in about 30 minutes, or 1.6 kilometres (1 mile). This is a fairly old, well-worn and easy to follow trail, albeit with only occasional red square markers on the trees. It makes its way uphill in a generally northwesterly direction, then curves generally southwesterly and downhill. After roughly half an hour you come to the signposted junction with the Brother's Creek Fire Access Road.

Turn left here and check out what remains of an old mill boiler house and steam sawmill site, built in 1912 but abandoned in 1913.

Continue downhill, and in 5 minutes you reach the junction with the BP/TCT trail at the power lines. Go down to your left, where in a couple of minutes you come to another signposted junction at Hadden Creek, about 1.5 to 2 hours after leaving Cleveland Dam. If you had earlier left a car at the upper Millstream Road trailhead, you now take the trail down to the right and in 5 minutes you are out on the road.

Otherwise, go to your left, following the BP/TCT/Skyline Trail into the woods as it parallels the power lines east to the Millstream Road/Craigmohr Drive junction. From here you retrace your steps back to Cleveland Dam and the parking lot. The return trip is about 45 minutes from the Hadden Creek junction.

BADEN-POWELL TRAIL

The Baden-Powell (BP) trail, named after Boy Scout founder Lord Baden-Powell, was completed in 1971 by Boy Scout and Girl Guide troops to mark BC's 100th birthday. It is a challenging and scenic 48-kilometre (30-mile) route that traverses the North Shore mountains from its western end near Horseshoe Bay in West Vancouver to Deep Cove in North Vancouver. There are some spectacular viewpoints and very pleasant, rewarding sections of trail, but also some especially demanding, strenuous ones.

In theory the entire BP trail could be covered in one very long day of 16 to 21 hours, depending on your fitness level and the number of daylight hours available, but this is not advisable. Fortunately there are many possible access points along the way to break it up into more manageable chunks of several hours each. I have divided the route into four segments, each about 12 kilometres (7.5 miles) long. For all but the first one, from the western end to Cypress Bowl, I have also provided an intermediate access/departure point, to shorten the hike if so desired.

The four segments, with time estimates, are:
- Western end to Cypress Bowl (5 to 7 hours);
- Cypress Bowl to Cleveland Dam (4 to 5 hours);
- Grouse Mountain to Lynn Canyon (3.5 to 4.5 hours);
- Lynn Canyon to Deep Cove (3.5 to 4.5 hours).

The first segment is by far the most challenging one, with its elevation gain of just over 1,000 metres (3,300 feet), and should only be attempted by experienced hikers in good physical condition.

Winter snow conditions on Black Mountain, Cypress and

Hollyburn shorten the hiking season for the two West Vancouver segments, while the two North Vancouver ones are good much of the year, depending on the severity of winter season snowfalls.

The annual Knee Knackering North Shore Trail Run, which follows this route almost exactly, has a website, www.kneeknacker. com, with a detailed course description, course profile and course map under the "Race Info/Course" tab. It may be humbling to know that the winners finish the whole course in just under 5 hours, with the laggards finishing in under 10 hours.

Navigating the BP trail itself is relatively straightforward in most places. The entire trail is well marked with orange "BP" fleur-de-lis triangles on the trees. Also, at major trail junctions there are signposts with distances and estimated completion times. Many signposts in the last segment have small maps on them, thanks to a 2006 project by the North Shore Mountain Bike Association.

Since these four are all one-way hikes, car transportation or public transit should be arranged for both ends.

14 ▸ Baden-Powell #1, Western End to Cypress Bowl

> **Elevation gain:** 1,087 metres (3,570 feet)
> **High point:** 1,217 metres (3,990 feet)
> **Season:** July to October
> **Topographical map:** North Vancouver 92G06
> **Hiking time:** 5 to 7 hours, including lunch
> Dog-friendly

Starting from the west, this first segment of the Baden-Powell (BP) is by far the most challenging and demanding, with its long slog up to Eagle Bluff. It's also the most rewarding, with a myriad of picturesque little sub-alpine lakes and spectacular vistas from both Eagle Bluff and Black Mountain. The hike takes you into Nelson Canyon Park and along Whyte Creek, after which you join the original BP trail heading up to Eagle Bluff and Black Mountain before descending to the Cypress Bowl Alpine (downhill) ski area pay parking lot.

Note that with the completion of the new Highway 1/99 Eagleridge Bypass in early 2009, it is possible to use the original Black Mountain trailhead again as an alternative (albeit a less desirable one) to the newer Nelson Canyon/Whyte Creek approach. You reach the former by taking the Eagleridge Exit 2 from Highway 1 in West Vancouver and pulling into a small, gravel parking area on your right a couple of minutes later. The Black Mountain Trail sign marks the trailhead, from which you walk up a gravel trail for about five minutes before going under the new Highway 99 overpass at Larson Creek. You then continue up the original BP trail, alongside the highway at first, before soon heading into the forest.

This hike is best done in mid-summer to early fall, long after the snow melts and before the fall rains start, as higher level sections of the trail can be muddy and slippery in places.

From Highway 1 in West Vancouver, you reach the trailhead by taking Exit 4, then turning left onto Westport Road. Go straight through at the four-way stop and follow Westport Road for about 1.5 kilometres (1 mile), going under the highway, before coming to a small, gravel parking area off to the right. Arrange car transportation for both ends of this hike.

You begin by walking past the yellow gate, along the winding gravel road and under the highway. Keep going straight ahead at the first Trans Canada Trail (TCT) sign, then turn right into the woods at a TCT (East) signpost a couple of minutes later. Following the winding uphill trail you soon hear Nelson Creek on your left.

About 15 to 20 minutes from your car you leave the main trail by going down to your left at a marked junction with a large red cedar stump. In about 5 minutes this meandering trail leads to the Nelson Creek crossing on a sturdy footbridge built in 2008.

This recently improved trail now follows Whyte Creek west. After a series of three boardwalks you come to a signposted junction near Whyte Lake. Continue straight ahead up the slope then downhill for a couple of minutes to reach the junction with the original BP route coming up from the old Eagleridge trailhead. Turn right here and head up the wide, rocky BP.

As it heads into the forest the trail gradually becomes more of a dirt path, crossing a small creek several times, then crossing Nelson Creek before beginning a steep ascent up the rock slide area. This part of the trail is not as well marked, but stay to your right, watching for orange flags on trees, small rock cairns and faint paint marks on boulders. As the grade steepens, carefully pick your way up among the large boulders. As you get closer to the top, still on the right-hand side, a dirt trail becomes more evident. You pass two false summits before finally reaching 1,094-metre (3,590-foot) Eagle Bluff.

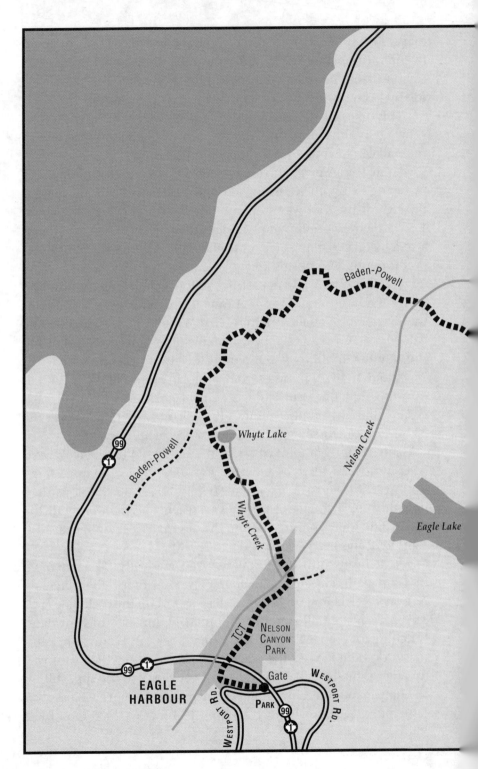

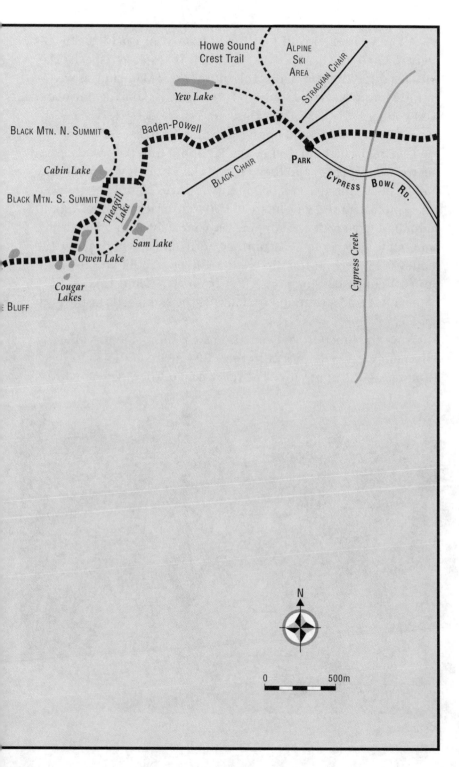

Allow yourself two to four hours from your car to get to this point, a good lunch stop. This viewpoint is absolutely spectacular, with magnificent views across the entire Lower Mainland, as well as east to Mount Baker and south to Point Roberts. Looking down and west you see Eagle Lake, Eagle Harbour, Whyte Lake, Horseshoe Bay, over to Bowen Island and up the Sunshine Coast.

Leaving Eagle Bluff, follow the BP uphill into the woods, passing the Cougar Lakes and then Owen Lake, both on your right. The trail through this area can be muddy in places. Shortly after Owen Lake you reach the 1,217-metre (3,990-foot) Black Mountain south summit, a large rock outcropping on your right with a 360-degree panoramic view. From here continue north and downhill about 190 metres (625 feet) on the dirt trail to the boardwalk and the signposted Cabin Lake junction. The very pretty Cabin Lake itself, a popular but cold swimming spot during the summer, is just over to your left.

From the junction you can also take a short side trip of about 250 metres (820 feet) north to the 1,224-metre (4,015-foot) Black Mountain north summit (a.k.a. Yew Lake Lookout), where you are

Summertime at Cabin Lake.

treated to views of the Lions, the Sea to Sky Highway and as far north as the Tantalus Range.

Back at the junction take the boardwalk east for about 100 metres (330 feet) then turn left to follow the Baden-Powell "To Base Area Parking Lot" sign. This descent leads you down a fairly steep, switch-backing trail to the Cypress Bowl parking lot in 35 to 45 minutes.

Looking down to Eagle Lake and Eagle Harbour from Eagle Bluff.

15 ▸ Baden-Powell #2, Cypress Bowl to Cleveland Dam

> **Elevation gain:** 150 metres (490 feet)
> **High point:** 1,070 metres (3,500 feet)
> **Season:** July to October
> **Topographical map:** North Vancouver 92G06
> **Hiking time:** 4 to 5 hours
> Dog-friendly

After initially rising up to the Hollyburn Peak turnoff, this second segment of the Baden-Powell (BP) is almost all downhill. It takes you from the Cypress Bowl Alpine (downhill) ski area to Cleveland Dam in North Vancouver. You descend through a variety of forested terrain, followed by a short trek across the top of the British Properties, then finally cross Cleveland Dam, where you are treated to views of Capilano Lake, the Lions and Grouse Mountain. (A midway access point is at upper Millstream Road in West Vancouver, reached by taking Exit 11 from Highway 1, going north on Crosscreek Road, left onto Chartwell Drive, then onto Millstream, staying left on Millstream to park just past Henlow Road.) It is best done in mid-summer to early fall, long after the snow melts and before the fall rains start, as higher-level sections of the trail can be muddy and slippery in places.

From Highway 1 in West Vancouver you reach the trailhead

by taking Exit 8 for Cypress Park and following Cypress Bowl Road 14 kilometres (8.5 miles) up to the Alpine ski area pay parking lot. Arrange for car transportation to Cypress Bowl and either another car or public transit for the Cleveland Dam (or Millstream Road) end.

There has been some rerouting of trails due to the 2010 Olympics construction, but begin by following the "Baden-Powell Trail to Hollyburn Mtn" sign from the trailhead just behind the Ski Patrol building. Follow these signs uphill as they lead you east and into the woods. You now gradually gain elevation on an easy-to-follow, undulating forest path through large second-growth fir and cedar. In the first half hour there are two crossings of Cypress Creek tributaries that could be problematic if spring runoff levels are high.

Also, the trail is quite rooty, so is slippery when wet. There are some muddy patches as you approach the signposted Hollyburn Peak turnoff (see hike #6), just under an hour from the start. Stay right at that junction, heading gradually downhill and alternating between forest cover and open areas.

After another 20 minutes or so you emerge into a clearing at the power lines, with Fourth Lake and the warming hut on your right. Continue straight across the clearing under the power lines to follow the BP east and into the woods. Here you begin heading downhill on Upper Wells Gray, one of the major cross-country ski trails. In about 15 minutes you reach a bench overlooking Hollyburn Lodge and First Lake. Continue down the ski trail, passing the first couple of signposted junctions. After about 15 minutes from the bench you turn left at a signposted junction to follow the BP downhill on a short, narrow, rocky section, with views of Indian Arm and Mount Baker off to the east. Go left at the next signposted junction and left again at the orange marker on a tree to follow the BP into the woods.

Continuing downhill, you pass an access trail to Blue Gentian Lake (a possible side trip if you have an extra few minutes; otherwise, see hike #8), then reach a large clearing, the site of the former Westlake Ski Lodge, which was originally moved piecemeal from West Lake in 1938 but which burned to the ground over 20 years ago. Follow the BP sign left into the woods and continue downhill, passing a second, shorter—only 300 metres (980 feet)—access trail

BADEN-POWELL TRAIL

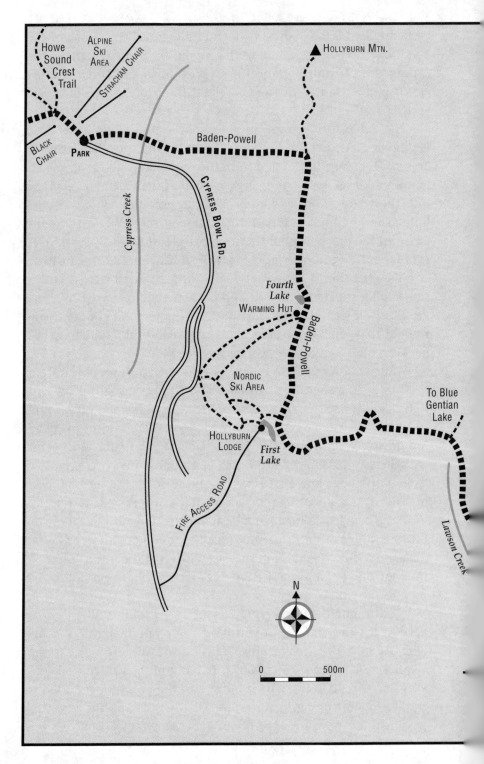

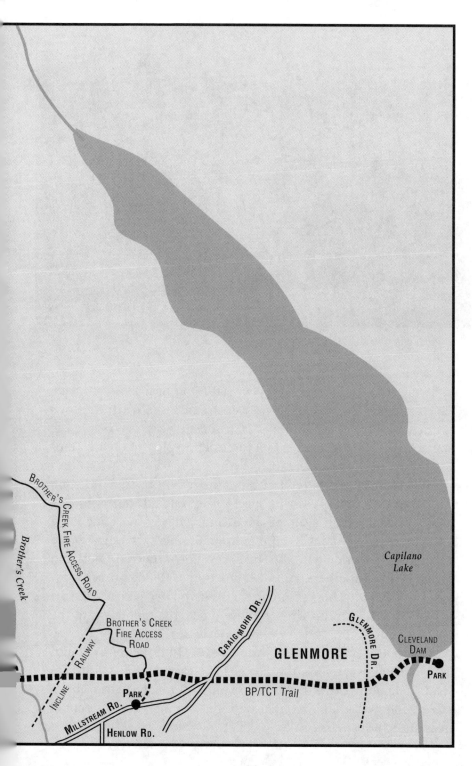

Hollyburn Lodge and First Lake from the Baden-Powell Trail.

to Blue Gentian Lake. Soon to your right you hear Lawson Creek, which parallels the trail all the way down until you reach the power lines. Be wary of steep drop-offs in some places. Just before the power lines, take the marked trail to the left to pick up the BP/Trans Canada Trail (TCT) heading east.

Stay right on the BP/TCT at the Brother's Creek Trail junction, cross Brother's Creek, with its spectacular waterfall during spring runoff, and stay right again at the Incline Railway trail junction a few minutes later. About 20 minutes from Brother's Creek you reach a signposted junction with the Fire Access Road. Stay right here and go downhill to another signposted junction at Hadden Creek, now about three to four hours from the start. If you had earlier left a car at the upper Millstream Drive trailhead, take the trail down to the right and out to the road.

Otherwise, you go left, following the BP/TCT/Skyline Trail into the woods as it parallels the power lines east. At the Millstream Road/Craigmohr Drive intersection you go through a green metal gate to follow the BP east as it descends through the residential areas of the British Properties.

At Glenmore Drive, pick up the trail directly across the street as it heads into the woods again. There is a brief uphill followed by a fairly steep but short downhill before you emerge onto a gravel road. Go right here, following the winding gravel road all the way downhill until you reach Cleveland Dam, about 45 minutes to an hour from the Hadden Creek junction. The parking lot and wash-rooms are just a couple of minutes ahead.

16 ▸ Baden-Powell #3, Grouse Mountain to Lynn Canyon

> **Elevation gain:** 216 metres (700 feet)
> **High point:** 490 metres (1,600 feet)
> **Season:** April to November
> **Topographical map:** North Vancouver 92G06
> **Hiking time:** 3.5 to 4.5 hours
> Dog-friendly

You will find this third segment of the Baden-Powell (BP), through second-growth forest along the lower slopes of Grouse Mountain and Mount Fromme, to be quite rewarding, particularly from Mosquito Creek east. There are lots of ups and downs along the way, but no major elevation gains, and many sections of upgraded trail. Although the last segment ended at Cleveland Dam, we will forgo the mile-long slog up Nancy Greene Way and start at the base of the Grouse Mountain Skyride (at the start of the Grouse Grind), finishing at the Lynn Canyon Park suspension bridge. (A midway access point is at the top of St. Marys Avenue, reached by driving north on Lonsdale from Highway 1, turning right on Braemar, left on St. Georges, right on Balmoral and left on St. Marys.)

From Highway 1 in North Vancouver, take Exit 14 to go north on Capilano Road. Follow it past Cleveland Dam and up Nancy Greene Way to the free gravel parking lot on your right (or the pay lot on your left) as you approach the Grouse Mountain Skyride. Arrange either car or public transit for both ends of this hike.

Begin by heading uphill and east from the trailhead gate, passing the Grouse Grind turnoff on your left in about 5 minutes. You continue steadily uphill on the BP for the next 20 to 30 minutes before the trail levels out somewhat. Over the next half hour or so you pass two signposted junctions for the old British Columbia Mountaineering Club (BCMC) trail up Grouse and cross two tributaries of MacKay Creek (without footbridges, so take care if water levels are high). About 10 minutes after passing a signposted junction for the 150-metre (490-foot) trail that goes down to Skyline Drive, you follow the BP signs down to a major footbridge across the sometimes-tumultuous Mosquito Creek canyon.

Immediately after the bridge, there is a signposted junction for the 250-metre (820-foot) trail that goes down to Prospect Road, but you follow the BP left and uphill, passing two large, green water towers on your right. About 20 minutes from Mosquito Creek you come to a bench with a fine view of Burrard Inlet, Vancouver and beyond. This is roughly the halfway point of the hike, approximately two hours from the start.

If you had earlier left a car at St. Marys, you now take the St. Georges Trail down to your right about 10 metres (30 feet) past the bench. Follow the red markers on the trees for about 10 minutes downhill until you emerge at the power lines. Here you go left and almost immediately you see ahead the gate at the top of St. Marys. Just past this gate, go to your right and downhill on St. Marys to your car.

Otherwise, continue your trek east along this very pleasant section of the BP for another hour or more on your way to Lynn Canyon. About 25 minutes past Kilmer Creek you emerge onto Mountain Highway (now the old Grouse Mountain Road at this point). Pick up the BP directly across the road and follow the signs downhill, eventually going down several flights of stairs, to reach the Lynn Headwaters access road about 20 minutes after leaving Mountain Highway.

Go right here and follow this road for about 15 minutes out to the stop sign at the Lynn Valley Road/Dempsey Road intersection. Go to your left at the BP signpost near the Fire Warning sign,

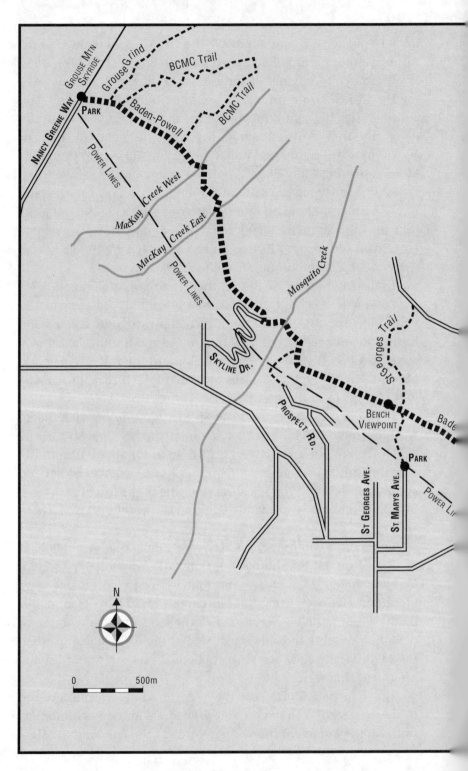

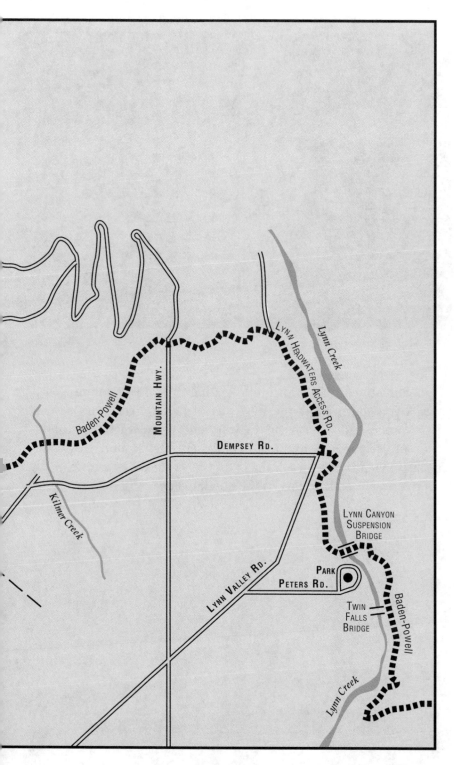

Looking north up Lynn Creek from the Baden-Powell Trail.

following the dirt trail down into Lynn Canyon. This winding path leads you south along the west side of Lynn Creek, with several boardwalks and stairs along the way, before you reach the suspension bridge about 20 minutes from the last intersection. Go up the stairs to your right to reach the Lynn Canyon Ecology Centre, Lynn Canyon Café, washrooms and the parking area.

17 ▸ Baden-Powell #4, Lynn Canyon to Deep Cove

Elevation gain: 380 metres (1,240 feet)
High point: 430 metres (1,400 feet)
Season: April to November
Topographical map: North Vancouver 92G06 and
Port Coquitlam 92G07
Hiking time: 3.5 to 4.5 hours
Dog-friendly

This fourth and final segment of the Baden-Powell (BP) trail takes you across two impressive river canyons, the Lynn and the Seymour. It also includes one of the BP's more strenuous uphill sections, followed by a very satisfying downhill ramble toward a Deep Cove lookout point, with lots of creeks and footbridges the rest of the way. The hike starts at the Lynn Canyon Park suspension bridge and finishes at Deep Cove. (A midway access point is at Hyannis Drive, reached by taking Exit 22 from Highway 1 in North Vancouver, going east on Mount Seymour Parkway, turning left onto Berkley Road and left again onto Hyannis at the top of Berkley.)

From Highway 1 in North Vancouver, take Exit 19 to go north on Lynn Valley Road. Soon after the shopping centre and the lights at Mountain Highway you pass a Royal Bank, then turn right on

Peters Road to enter Lynn Canyon Park. Arrange either car or public transit for both ends of this hike.

You begin at the BP signpost on the west side of the suspension bridge. Cross the bridge, go along the boardwalk and follow the BP to the right toward the Twin Falls Bridge, where you may see cliff jumpers in the summer months. Take a minute to admire the view of the falls, then continue south along the east side of Lynn Creek. This is a winding dirt trail, rooty in places, but with several boardwalks. About 10 minutes from Twin Falls, part way

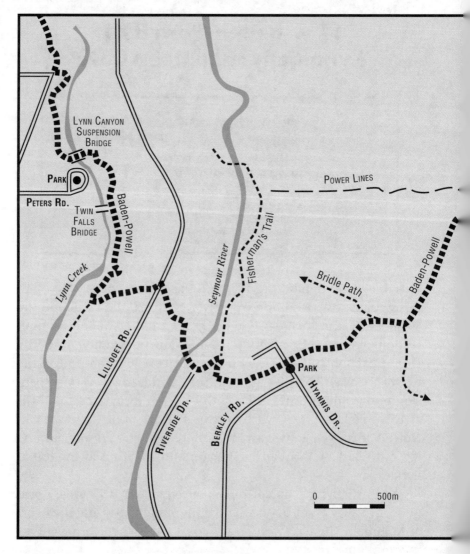

along an elevated boardwalk, there is a nice little beach just off to your right.

Shortly after that boardwalk you begin your climb out of Lynn Canyon. About 10 to 15 minutes later you reach a BP signposted junction at the top of the hill. Go left to follow the BP northeast to Lillooet Road. Pick up the trail across the road and continue southeast toward the Seymour River, passing the Richard Juryn Trail signposts (see hike #21). A few minutes later carefully follow the switchbacking trail downhill, then descend a steep flight of stairs to the

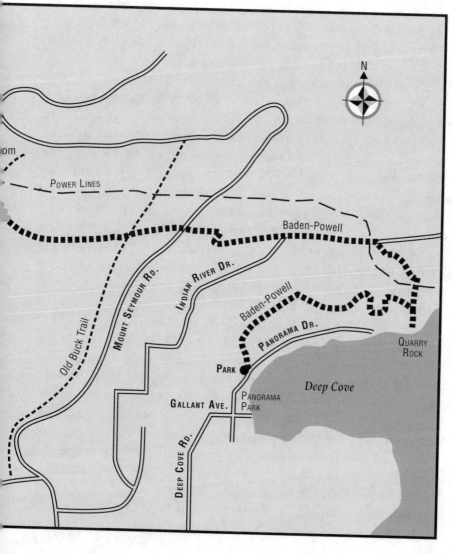

pipe bridge over the canyon. After a short uphill on the other side, you see a footbridge out to Riverside Drive on your right, but you turn left to follow the BP north. At a signposted junction with the Fisherman's Trail a couple of minutes later, go right and follow the BP alongside Canyon Creek up to Hyannis Drive.

Arriving at Hyannis, about 1.25 to 1.5 hours from the suspension bridge, pick up the BP on the other side of the road (unless you had earlier left a car here in order to complete this segment another day). Continue along the creek, going steadily uphill until you meet the Bridle Path trail at a footbridge 15 to 20 minutes from Hyannis. Go right here, on the joint BP/Bridle Path trail. At the next signposted T-junction where the trails part, about 70 metres (230 feet) ahead, you turn left to follow the BP north.

Soon you leave the creek behind and the BP starts a fairly steep climb, not unlike part of the Grouse Grind. After about a half hour or more of steady uphill plodding the trail levels out a bit near its signposted intersection with the top of Severed D (a.k.a. Good Samaritan), a good place for a water stop. Continuing east along the BP for about five minutes you reach its signposted junction with the Mushroom Parking Lot trail (a possible side trip if you have an extra half hour or so; otherwise, see hike #25). Continue east along the BP until you reach its junction with Old Buck trail. Turn left up Old Buck for about 80 metres (260 feet), then right to continue east on the BP. This section of the BP is a pleasant, winding forest path that heads gradually downhill for the next few minutes until it emerges at Mount Seymour Road.

Pick up the BP directly across the road and follow this very agreeable trail until you reach Indian River Drive. Here you go left and walk along the road for 500 metres (1,640 feet), passing under power lines just before reaching the BP signpost on your right. Take this trail downhill and back into the forest. In about five minutes you reach a wide dirt road; continue straight ahead to follow the BP downhill at the signpost. After another five minutes or so you come out at the power lines again. Continue south directly across the open space and just to the right of the transmission tower to pick up the BP as it heads downhill.

In another couple of minutes you see Quarry Rock, sometimes referred to as Grey Rock, in a clearing directly ahead of you.

Baden-Powell Trail between Mount Seymour Road and Indian River Drive.

A hundred years ago Granite Quarries Ltd. was located just below this lookout, and operated from 1908 to 1924. Take a break here to enjoy the spectacular, 180-degree views of Deep Cove, Indian Arm and beyond. When you're ready to continue, take the BP trail out to your left (west). At a steady pace you reach Deep Cove and the end of the 48-kilometre (30-mile) Baden-Powell trail in about half an hour.

NORTH VANCOUVER

18 ▸ Capilano Canyon

> **Elevation gain:** minimal
> **High point:** 150 metres (490 feet)
> **Season:** Year-round
> **Topographical map:** North Vancouver 92G06
> **Hiking time:** 2.5 to 3.5 hours
> Dog-friendly

Here is an all-weather jaunt that provides a comprehensive introduction to both the popular and the less-travelled trails of Capilano
River Regional Park, including visits to the Capilano River Fish
Hatchery and some giant old-growth Douglas firs. The hike takes
you from Cleveland Dam down the west side of the Capilano River,
across the river for a loop down the lesser-known east side, then
back up to the hatchery and across the river again for your return
to Cleveland Dam. There are several opportunities along the way to
shorten the hike, depending on how much time you have.

From Highway 1 in North Vancouver, take Exit 14 to go north
on Capilano Road. Follow it up to the paved parking lot on your
left, just past Clements Avenue but before Nancy Greene Way heads
up toward Grouse Mountain.

This lovely, 160-hectare (395-acre) park was created in 1926 and is administered by Metro Vancouver. The river was originally known as Homulchesan, as was the native village at its mouth. It was later renamed after the great Squamish chief Kia'palano, who died about 1875 and was buried on the Mission Reserve in North Vancouver.

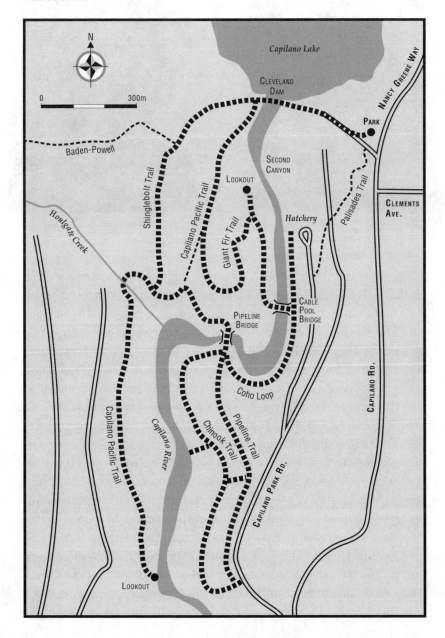

Fishing in the Capilano River Cable Pool, downstream from the Cable Pool Bridge.

Begin by walking across Cleveland Dam, admiring the views of Capilano Lake, the Lions and Grouse Mountain up on your right, then the awe-inspiring spillway and vertical canyon walls to your left. The dam was completed in 1954 and named after Ernest A. Cleveland, the first chief commissioner of the Greater Vancouver Water District from 1926 to 1952. Across the dam you see two gravel roads on your left. The lower one will be your return route, so take the upper one with the BP (Baden-Powell trail) signplate.

Follow the BP uphill, turning left in about five minutes at the signposted Shinglebolt Trail junction. Take the Shinglebolt downhill, going left at the bottom of the wooden steps. About 40 metres (130 feet) farther on go right up a short tangle of tree roots. Next you turn right down a wooden staircase, and follow red markers on the trees down a short trail. Go right at the bench, then down some stairs to a signposted junction with the Capilano Pacific Trail.

Go right here and cross the reinforced footbridge over Houlgate Creek. The creek was named after R.K. Houlgate, a Vancouver Board of Trade member and part of a syndicate that constructed a long, wooden flume to transport shingle bolts (long, wedge-shaped blocks of cedar from which shakes and shingles were cut) from a steam sawmill at Sisters Creek, a tributary of the Capilano, all the way down the river to Burrard Inlet in the early 1900s.

Continue south following the scenic Capilano Pacific, the route of the 8.5-kilometre (5-mile) Coho Walk each September from Cleveland Dam to Ambleside Park in West Vancouver, for 10 to 15 minutes, until you reach an observation platform on your left with a dramatic view of the canyon. From the lookout return back upstream to the Houlgate Creek bridge.

After crossing the bridge, follow the Capilano Pacific along to a signposted junction where you go right, down the Shinglebolt Trail and across a gravel road to reach the Pipeline Bridge river crossing. On the east side, take the Chinook Trail up to your right and follow it south as it parallels the river. Five to ten minutes later, at a Trans Canada Trail signpost, you can take a short, dirt side trail down to a sunny, level but rocky area next to the river. Returning to the main trail, about ten minutes later you reach a yellow gate that marks the junction of the Chinook Trail with Capilano Park Road and the Pipeline Trail. Go left here to follow the gravel Pipeline Trail back north into the woods.

Emerging at the Pipeline Bridge junction again, go right to take the Coho Loop trail as it winds its way north along the east side of the river canyon, passing the Cable Pool on the way. Next you see the Cable Pool Bridge ahead on your left. Leaving this for the moment, stay to the right to visit the fish hatchery and take in its educational displays and check for activity in its fish ladders.

If you are short of time, the Palisades Trail just east of the hatchery provides a convenient, albeit fairly steep, one-kilometre (half-mile) shortcut back up to the parking lot. Otherwise, return to cross the Cable Pool Bridge, watching downstream for fishermen trying their luck in the deep pools below.

Across the bridge, turn right and follow this trail upstream for about five minutes to the Second Canyon Viewpoint lookout area, with its spectacular view of the dam spillway. There are also storyboards that outline the early history of the canyon and identify the various salmon species that use the river and the hatchery fish ladders. From here retrace your steps about 60 metres (200 feet) and take the Giant Fir Trail to your right and uphill. In the next five minutes or so you pass some massive old-growth Douglas firs and finally reach the ancient Grandpa Capilano, 2.4 metres (8 feet) in diameter and more than 60 metres (200 feet) high.

Continue up this trail, turning right at its junction with the Capilano Pacific a few minutes later. Now follow that trail on its gradual ascent up to Cleveland Dam and return to the parking lot.

The "Grandpa Capilano" Douglas fir in Capilano Canyon.

19 ▶ Norvan Falls

Elevation gain: 190 metres (620 feet)
High point: 370 metres (1,200 feet)
Season: May to November
Topographical map: North Vancouver 92G06
Hiking time: 4 to 5 hours, including lunch
Dog-friendly

This rewarding, 14- to 15-kilometre (8.5- to 9-mile) return trip through the lush rainforest of Lynn Headwaters Regional Park features only gradual elevation changes along the way to the impressive Norvan Falls. The hike takes you along a route with abundant evidence of early 1900s' logging activities to a viewpoint below Norvan Falls, then back to the trailhead either directly or via a slightly longer Lynn Loop Trail circuit.

From Highway 1 in North Vancouver, take Exit 19 to go north on Lynn Valley Road. After passing a shopping centre then the lights at Mountain Highway, watch for signs for Lynn Headwaters Park (passing the turnoff for Lynn Canyon Park) and park in the small paved lot at the end of the access road or in either of the two overflow lots. The park is administered by Metro Vancouver and was reopened to the public in 1985 after being closed since 1928 as part of the North Shore watershed system.

Begin by taking the footbridge across Lynn Creek and going

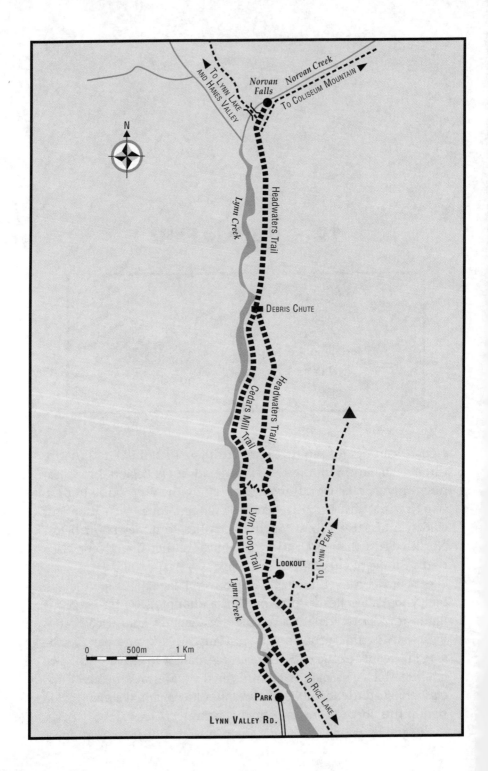

left at the trailhead kiosk (the trail coming down from the right is your Lynn Loop return route). On this wide, gravel Cedars Mill Trail you see occasional remnants of logging activity, such as an old four-wheel log transporter at the 0.5 kilometre mark, more rusted machinery at the signposted Cedars Mill Site and of course the ubiquitous massive old-growth stumps.

After 20 to 25 minutes along this very pleasant trail you reach a short connector path up to the Lynn Loop/Headwaters Trail, but continue to your left, following Lynn Creek north. At the end of a boardwalk, stay straight ahead rather than going up the stairs to the right. The trail now narrows and becomes rougher and more winding, but is still very easy to follow, even without the yellow markers on the trees. At about 4 kilometres (2.5 miles), 45 to 55 minutes from the start, you reach a large clearing and debris chute. The nearby Mount Fromme towers up to the west and the creek access here provides a good spot for a break.

Continue north, now on the Headwaters Trail, from the signpost at the top of the debris chute. Soon you see stretches of the deteriorating old corduroy logging road and additional cookhouse relics from a logging camp of a century ago. The trail now becomes a little steeper and rockier in places, but is also farther from the creek, so you are truly in the peace and quiet of the forest. Some sections can become quite muddy during rainy periods.

About 40 to 50 minutes from the debris chute you pass the signposted turnoff to your right for the Coliseum Mountain hike. This 7-hour trip has over 1,000 metres (3,300 feet) more elevation gain and is suitable only for experienced and well-prepared hikers. Just ahead you reach Norvan Creek. The steel suspension bridge leads north to a very rugged trail to Lynn Lake, again suitable only for experienced and well-prepared hikers, or to the challenging Hanes Valley Crossover route to Grouse Mountain, with another 1,000 metres (3,300 feet) elevation gain and roughly another 5.5 to 6 hours one way. For today, take the short access trail about 5 minutes upstream and find a creekside lunchtime viewpoint of the falls.

To begin your return trip, retrace your steps back to the debris chute. For a little more variety and elevation gain, stay left at the signpost to continue on the upper Headwaters Trail rather than returning via the lower Cedars Mill Trail. The upper trail is longer

Norvan Falls.

and rougher, but is also more like a continuation of the 3-kilometre (1.8-mile) woodsy, peaceful trail from Norvan Creek to this point.

About 35 to 45 minutes from the debris chute, just after a fenced valley lookout point, you reach the signposted junction with the switchback connector path down to the Cedars Mill Trail, another option for your return if you are running short of time. Otherwise, continue along what is now the upper part of the Lynn Loop Trail. After about 15 minutes you pass a signposted Lynn Valley Viewpoint, a few minutes up a steep side trail on your left.

In another 15 minutes or so you pass the signposted turnoff to the Lynn Peak trail on your left. From here the Lynn Loop Trail continues its descent for another few minutes, now as a wide gravel path, before meeting the connector trail from Rice Lake in the Lower Seymour Conservation Reserve (see hike #20). Go downhill to your right for another 5 minutes or so until you come to the trailhead kiosk, where you go left and across the Lynn Creek footbridge back to the parking lot.

20 ▸ Lynn Creek and Rice Lake

> **Elevation gain:** 50 metres (165 feet)
> **High point:** 200 metres (650 feet)
> **Season:** Year-round
> **Topographical map:** North Vancouver 92G06
> **Hiking time:** 1.5 to 2 hours
> Dogs not permitted on Rice Lake Loop Trail

This short, easy, year-round hike treats you to a very pleasant stroll alongside Lynn Creek and a visit to scenic, tranquil Rice Lake, which abounds with both fishing opportunities and a history of early 1900s' logging activities. You start in Lynn Headwaters Regional Park, going south along Lynn Creek, up to the man-made Rice Lake in the Lower Seymour Conservation Reserve (LSCR) and back to Lynn Headwaters.

From Highway 1 in North Vancouver, take Exit 19 to go north on Lynn Valley Road. After passing a shopping centre then the lights at Mountain Highway, watch for signs for Lynn Headwaters Park (passing the turnoff for Lynn Canyon Park) and park in the small paved lot at the end of the access road or in either of the two overflow lots. The park is administered by Metro Vancouver and was reopened to the public in 1985 after being closed since 1928 as part of the North Shore watershed system.

Begin on the Varley Trail at the entrance to the paved lot or down the stairs from either of the overflow lots. This trail, named after renowned Group of Seven artist and former Lynn Valley resident Frederick Varley, connects Lynn Headwaters with the LSCR. You head back southeast along this well-maintained trail, with its long boardwalks over marshy areas and Lynn Creek close by on your left. There is a short uphill stretch before you emerge onto a gravel road. At Rice Lake Road go left to take the large, sturdy footbridge across Lynn Creek, now deep in the canyon below.

Go straight ahead up a gentle slope for about five minutes to a large, grassy, open area with a pagoda, picnic tables, water fountain and toilets. This area, with its nearby parking lot at the top of Lillooet Road, is an excellent connecting point to several longer excursions: Lynn Canyon and the Baden-Powell trail to the south (see hikes #16 and #17); the LSCR trail system to the east (see hikes #23 and #24); and the Fisherman's Trail or Seymour Valley Trailway to the north (see hike #22).

Saving those for other days, you follow the signs to Rice Lake, about 500 metres (1,650 feet) north. Stay on the trail to the left as

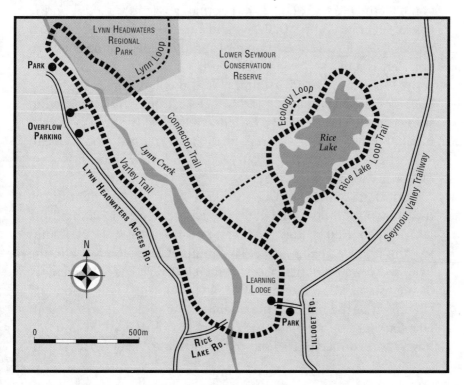

Looking across Rice Lake to Mount Seymour.

you pass the Learning Lodge, rather than going to the right on the paved Seymour Valley Trailway, and turn right at the signposted junction for Rice Lake a couple of minutes later. Immediately to your left is a flume display and storyboard illustrating how in the early 1900s long wooden flumes were used to transport shingle bolts (long, wedge-shaped blocks of cedar from which shakes and shingles were cut) from Rice Lake down to Moodyville. That settlement, founded on Burrard Inlet in 1863, was named Moodyville in 1872 after sawmill owner Sewell Moody and was renamed the City of North Vancouver in 1907.

Continue along the wide Rice Lake Trail, turning right at the next junction to take the Loop Trail counter-clockwise around the lake. In about 50 metres (165 feet) you reach a lovely viewpoint looking north across the lake. Five minutes later you come to the Douglas Mowat Fisheries Project, which is dedicated to the memory of the former MLA, founder of the BC Paraplegic Association and champion of the rights of the disabled. The project is an excellent lake lookout and a popular fishing spot. The signposted junction has a short connector trail out to the Seymour Valley Trailway, but you continue north on the Loop Trail around the lake, noticing the abundance of viewpoints and fishing spots along the way.

Just after passing a second connector trail to the Seymour Valley Trailway, you come to the lake outflow point and another storyboard. It describes the use of Rice Lake by the Hastings Shingle Manufacturing Company in the early 1900s to store cedar shingle bolts prior to their being transported on the flume line down to Moodyville. Next, the 400-metre (1,300-foot) unmarked Ecology Loop is worth a side trip, with a storyboard that provides some additional information on early 1900s' logging activity here. Back on the Loop Trail, a few minutes later you come to a signposted junction with a connector trail out to Lynn Headwaters, but unless you are in a hurry, stay to the left to continue around the lake.

In another few minutes there is a storyboard off to your right that describes how Rice Lake was converted by the City of North Vancouver in 1912 from a shingle bolt storage area to a drinking water reservoir, as backup to the Lynn Creek system. There is also a memorial here to the passengers and crew of Trans Canada Airlines flight 3, which crashed in 1947 on a remote area just west of Mount Elsay (visible to the north on a clear day) and was not found until 1994.

Now continue just down the hill to the next signposted junction to complete the circuit of this very pretty, serene little lake. You pass the flume display again before emerging at the connector trail. Here you turn right and follow this wide pathway northwest back into Lynn Headwaters Park.

About 10 minutes later you reach the Lynn Headwaters/LSCR Boundary signpost, where the Lynn Loop/Lynn Peak Trail heads up to the right, but you continue straight ahead for another 5 minutes or so until you come to the Lynn Headwaters trailhead kiosk. Norvan Falls (see hike #19) and several more ambitious hikes (Hanes Valley, Lynn Lake, Coliseum Mountain) originate from here, but today you go left and across the Lynn Creek footbridge back to the parking lot.

21 ▸ Richard Juryn Trail/ Old Lillooet Trail

Elevation gain: 170 metres (550 feet)
High point: 220 metres (720 feet)
Season: Year-round
Topographical map: North Vancouver 92G06
Hiking time: 1.75 to 2.25 hours
Dog-friendly

This all-season North Vancouver hike, with only moderate elevation gain, combines a loop around the scenic Richard Juryn Memorial Trail with a return trip on part of the historic Old Lillooet Trail south along Lynn Creek. It takes you from the trailhead at the top of Premier Street, around the Richard Juryn (RJ) trail, then over to Lynn Canyon via the Baden-Powell (BP) trail and back along Lynn Creek to the trailhead.

The Richard Juryn Trail is dedicated to the memory of Richard Juryn, who died October 7, 2007, in a tragic kayaking accident on Howe Sound. Richard was very involved in the community and had dreamed of building a trail network on the North Shore. His dream was realized with the construction of this trail through a massive effort by over 250 North Shore Mountain Bike Association and other volunteers on July 19, 2008.

From Highway 1 in North Vancouver, take Exit 22 (Lillooet

Road). Turn left at the light to drive north on Lillooet Road, then left at the next light onto Old Lillooet Road. Follow it around behind the Holiday Inn, then turn right onto Premier Street. Follow it north, going left at the Inter River Park sign, then right up a short hill to the Richard Juryn (RJ) trailhead sign at the end of the parking lot.

Begin by following the path north and clockwise around the playing field, noticing Grouse Mountain, Mount Fromme and Lynn Peak off in the distance. Watch for the RJ sign that directs you out of the playing field area and up Inter River Park Road to Lillooet Road. Go left on Lillooet Road, passing the North Shore Equestrian

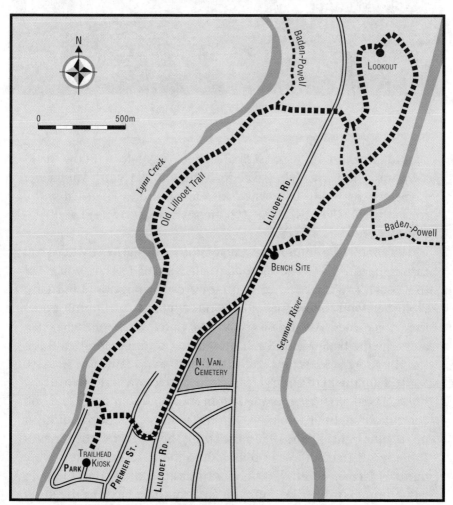

Mount Seymour's Power Lines Trail from the Richard Juryn Trail lookout.

Centre on your left. Just past Boal Chapel, stay left to follow the RJ signs up a short stretch of paved road through the North Vancouver Cemetery, rejoining Lillooet Road a few minutes later. Cross the road at the RJ signpost about 100 metres (330 feet) ahead and continue north.

In about 10 minutes you reach another RJ signpost where you turn right into the woods. About 50 metres (165 feet) in, you come to a bench and a viewpoint south toward Vancouver and Burnaby. From here you follow the wide, winding gravel path uphill under the power lines, reaching a small grassy area with another bench and a picnic table about 5 minutes later. Continue uphill and follow the RJ signs to its junction with the BP trail a few minutes later.

Pick up the RJ directly across the BP and follow it north into the forest. Three other trails branch off in the first few minutes, but you continue straight ahead, now with the sound of the Seymour River off to your right. About 10 minutes from the BP, follow the series of RJ signposts that lead you uphill and to the west. After a few more minutes there is another RJ signpost indicating a viewpoint to your left. From the top of the bluff you look south and east to the lower slopes of Mount Seymour. Return to the signpost and continue along the trail, following it west and downhill until you emerge at its junction with the BP about 5 minutes from the lookout point.

You could continue south from here directly across the BP to retrace your steps on the RJ back to the start, but an alternative route that provides some additional variety is to take the BP west to Lynn Canyon, then follow Lynn Creek south back to the RJ trailhead.

Go right on the BP for a couple of minutes before arriving at Lillooet Road. The BP, well marked with orange "BP" fleur-de-lis triangles on the trees, continues into the forest at the signpost across the road. Soon you hear Lynn Creek off in the distance, and in another few minutes you arrive at a signposted junction with the Old Lillooet Trail, named after an ill-fated old cattle trail built in the 1870s from Lillooet to Moodyville on the north shore of Burrard Inlet.

Here the BP continues downhill to the right, but you go left and south along this well-maintained trail. Soon you start your descent into Lynn Canyon. The trail is rather rocky and rooty in places, but does have some boardwalks across the marshy areas. In 20 to 25 minutes from the BP junction you have Lynn Creek close by on your right.

Before long the forest opens up and the trail levels out into a wide dirt path. Stay to the right, and in about another 10 minutes you come to a trail junction, with a footbridge across Lynn Creek on your right and a trail heading uphill to your left. Take the latter, checking the abundant nearby bushes for ripe blackberries during August. This trail leads you back past the Inter River Park playing field and to the parking lot in another 5 minutes.

22 ▸ Upper Fisherman's Trail

> **Elevation gain:** 140 metres (460 feet)
> **High point:** 250 metres (820 feet)
> **Season:** Most of the year
> **Topographical map:** North Vancouver 92G06
> **Hiking time:** 3.5 to 4 hours, including lunch
> Dogs not permitted on trail to Spur 4 Bridge

This scenic trail combines minimal elevation gain with magnificent mountain vistas as you make your way north along the banks of the Seymour River. The Seymour Valley was an off-limits watershed from 1928 to 1987, when it was reopened to the public as part of the Seymour Demonstration Forest, later renamed the Lower Seymour Conservation Reserve (LSCR) and administered by Metro Vancouver. The 12- to 14-kilometre (7.5- to 9-mile) round trip takes you from the trailhead at the top of Lillooet Road in North Vancouver, down the Homestead Trail, and along the Fisherman's Trail to the Spur 4 Bridge Mid-Valley Viewpoint, then back to your starting point by either of two return routes.

From Highway 1 in North Vancouver, take Exit 22 (Lillooet Road). Turn left at the light to drive north on Lillooet Road. Continue until you come to the gravel parking lot next to a water filtration plant construction area. This is not a pay lot, but watch for the signs telling you when the gates are locked for the night.

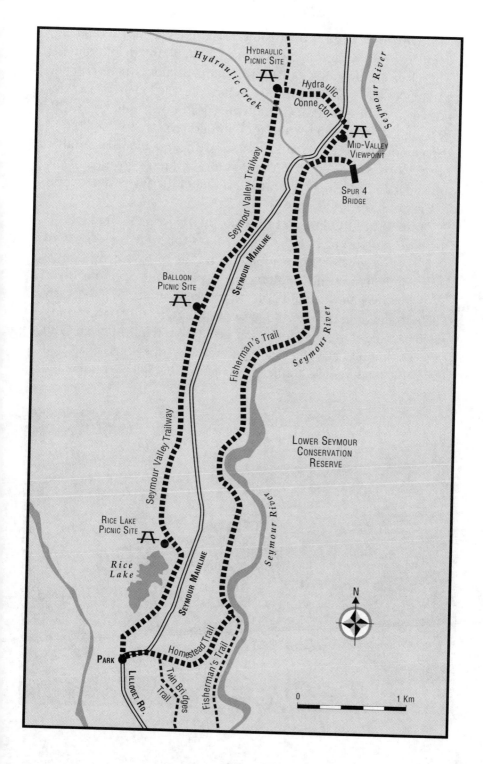

Nearby there is an Info Centre and Parks office, as well as a grassy, open area with a pagoda, picnic tables, water fountain and toilets.

You begin by going east on the footpath along the top of the parking lot and past the entrance to the construction area to a sign-posted junction for the two trails that lead down into the LSCR. Leaving the Twin Bridges trail for another day, stay to the left and descend on the very pleasant Homestead Trail for about 15 minutes or so, passing through an enchanted forest of moss-covered maple and alder and noticing the growing sound of the Seymour River off in the distance.

Turn left at the intersection with the Fisherman's Trail (this is the beginning of the no dogs area). Follow this wide, well-travelled trail, part of which is quite a long boardwalk over some wet areas, as it winds its way north along the banks of the Seymour River. Occasionally you see remnants of the logging days of the early 1900s in the form of large, old-growth stumps, many of which have since become nurse logs for newer generation trees. After an hour or so of minimal elevation gain you reach a wide gravel road that has occasional vehicle traffic going across the Spur 4 Bridge and beyond.

Runner Peak and Mount Elsay from the Mid-Valley Viewpoint picnic area.

A short side trip down the road will take you to the bridge itself, but to get to the Mid-Valley Viewpoint take the trail into the woods directly across the road. In about five minutes you arrive at your destination, a nice grassy area with toilets, picnic tables and a covered picnic area. Enjoy the views of Mount Seymour, Runner Peak and Mount Elsay across the valley to the east as you eat your lunch. You may be visited by the occasional raven looking for food scraps.

Now refreshed by your picnic lunch, follow the signs for the Seymour Valley Trailway via the Hydraulic Connector Trail (named after nearby Hydraulic Creek). This 400-metre (1,300-foot) trail leads west into the woods and crosses the Seymour Mainline Road, which is closed to the public. After a couple of minutes you see a signpost indicating the Butterfly Garden off to the right. A nearby storyboard explains how the area, once used as a bomb disposal site by the RCMP, has been transformed into a habitat for some 20 species of butterflies. Leaving the Butterfly Garden and continuing up the Connector Trail, you pass through another amazing enchanted forest where it seems as if almost every tree branch is draped with moss, a testimony to the area's heavy annual rainfall.

At this point you have two possibilities for your return trip to the Lillooet Road parking lot, with roughly equal return times. You can turn around here and return to the Mid-Valley Viewpoint, then retrace your steps back along the Fisherman's Trail and up the Homestead Trail to the parking lot.

Alternatively, you can continue up the Connector Trail to reach the Seymour Valley Trailway junction, where you go left. While this six-kilometre (four-mile) stretch of undulating paved road is rather uninspiring, it does have a couple of points of interest. After 25 to 30 minutes or so, you reach the Balloon Picnic Area (at Balloon Creek). A storyboard a few minutes ahead describes how in 1967 there was some experimental balloon logging salvage activity in this area. After about another half hour, you reach the Rice Creek Picnic Area. On the right-hand side of the road is a connector trail leading to the nearby Rice Lake Loop Trail. This trail could be an alternative way back if you have an extra hour or so to circle the very scenic Rice Lake (see hike #20 for guidance), then follow the signs from Rice Lake back to the Lillooet Road parking lot.

A little farther along the Trailway there is another Rice Lake connector trail, this one leading to the Douglas Mowat fishing wharf. A few metres ahead a storyboard marks the site of the original Rice Lake Road, circa 1910. It also gives some insight into homesteader S. Smith's use of this area as a pasture or corral for livestock until the 1930s. Continuing along the Trailway, you reach the parking lot area in another few minutes.

23 ▸ Seymour–Lynn Canyon Round Trip

> **Elevation gain:** 150 metres (490 feet)
> **High point:** 200 metres (650 feet)
> **Season:** Year-round
> **Topographical map:** North Vancouver 92G06
> **Hiking time:** 2.5 to 3.5 hours
> Dog-friendly

On this moderately strenuous but very satisfying hike, you pass through two lovely, forested North Vancouver parks and have the opportunity for a quick dip in both Lynn Creek and the Seymour River. The route takes you from the trailhead at Hyannis Drive down to the Seymour River, over to Lynn Canyon then back along the Seymour River and up to Hyannis.

From Highway 1 in North Vancouver, take Exit 22 (Mount Seymour Parkway). Going east on Mount Seymour Parkway, turn left at Berkley Road. At the top of Berkley turn left onto Hyannis Drive and park anywhere in that one-block section of Hyannis.

Begin by taking the signposted Baden-Powell (BP) trail on the south side of Hyannis, which leads you downhill alongside Canyon Creek and is well marked with orange "BP" fleur-de-lis triangles on the trees. You reach the Anglers Trail (a.k.a. Fisherman's Trail) signpost about 10 minutes from Hyannis. Go left here for another couple of minutes until you see the Riverside Drive trailhead. Just before a sturdy wooden footbridge that would lead you into the cul-de-sac, you go right and downhill again, crossing the surprisingly steep Seymour River canyon on a narrow pipe bridge.

Next is 10 to 15 minutes of uphill slogging as you first climb a long flight of 55 stairs, then follow the fairly steep trail as it switchbacks its way up before finally levelling out near a concrete pipeline.

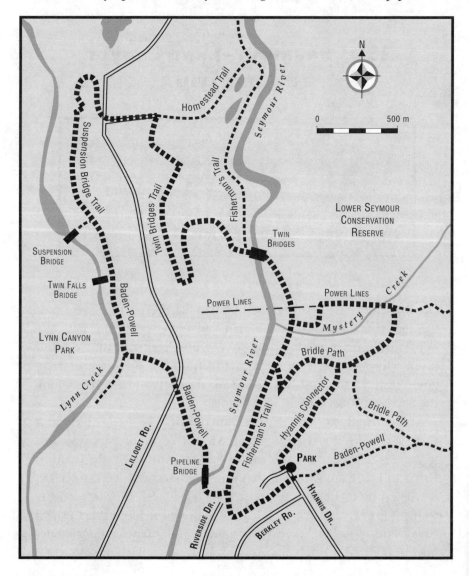

Follow the trail northwest under the power lines and straight ahead for another few minutes, past the signposted Richard Juryn Trail junctions (see hike #21), before arriving at Lillooet Road. The BP continues into the forest at a signpost immediately across the road. Soon you hear Lynn Creek off in the distance, and in about 10 minutes you arrive at a signposted junction with the Old Lillooet Trail to Premier Street. Here you go down to the right to descend into Lynn Canyon. Part way along the boardwalk across a marshy area, you see a small beach at the side of Lynn Creek. The beach is a good spot for a water stop and a rest at the water's edge.

Continue up Lynn Canyon for 10 to 15 minutes before you come to Twin Falls Bridge. In the summer months you may see cliff jumpers here. Don't cross the bridge, but continue up the east side of the canyon for another 10 to 15 minutes before coming to a sign for the suspension bridge on your left. A short detour across the suspension bridge will take you to the Lynn Canyon Ecology Centre and the Lynn Canyon Café building, with a concession and washrooms.

The BP continues across the suspension bridge, but you stay on the east side of Lynn Canyon all the way up. Once the trail levels out it becomes a wide, winding gravel path. Stay left at the water

A small Lynn Creek beach just off the Baden-Powell trail.

filtration plant construction area to continue going north. About 15 minutes from the suspension bridge you reach a grassy, open area with a pagoda, picnic tables, water fountain and toilets. This area is roughly the halfway point of the hike and another good spot for a rest. If time permits, a one-hour side trip might be the signposted trail to Rice Lake, about 500 metres (1,650 feet) north (see hike #20).

From the pagoda you go east toward the Info Centre and Parks office, then along the top of a gravel parking lot and past the construction area to a signposted junction for the two trails that lead down into the Lower Seymour Conservation Reserve. Leaving the Homestead Trail for another day, turn right and descend on the wide, gravel Twin Bridges Trail. About 25 minutes later you reach the Twin Bridges/Fisherman's Trail junction. Only one of the original two bridges remains (rebuilt in 2009); cross it and continue south along the east bank of the Seymour River. Note that a small sandy beach just below the bridge on the east side (when the river is low enough) can be reached by a set of concrete steps on your right.

There are three possibilities from here to return to Hyannis. The first and longest is the signposted junction with the Mystery Creek Trail about 5 minutes from the twin bridge. It is a fairly steep trail and you need to be alert for mountain bikers who may be descending. After about 10 minutes of uphill plodding you come out at the Power Lines Trail, where you turn right and continue uphill for another few minutes to the Mystery Creek footbridge. Turning right again immediately after the footbridge will take you back to the Hyannis Connector and out to Hyannis in another 15 to 20 minutes.

Alternatively, you can continue along the Fisherman's Trail for another few minutes after the Mystery Creek junction and turn up the signposted Bridle Path trail. This is a shorter, easier ascent than Mystery Creek. At the top, after 12 to 15 minutes of climbing, you go right and along a winding boardwalk, then right again at an unmarked T-junction with the Hyannis Connector out to Hyannis.

The third option is to continue along the Fisherman's Trail from the Bridle Path junction, enjoying more of the Seymour River canyon. In 10 to 15 minutes you reach its junction with the BP from Hyannis, just before the Riverside Drive trailhead. Here you go left and retrace your steps back up to Hyannis where you started.

24 ▸ Lower Seymour Conservation Reserve

Elevation gain: 130 metres (420 feet)
High point: 200 metres (650 feet)
Season: Year-round
Topographical map: North Vancouver 92G06
Hiking time: 2.5 to 3 hours
Dog-friendly

The Lower Seymour Conservation Reserve (LSCR), administered by Metro Vancouver, was once known as the Seymour Demonstration Forest. Part of the watershed from 1928 to 1987, this 5,668-hectare (14,000-acre) forest was reopened to the public and now offers diverse hiking opportunities through a landscape of forested slopes and spectacular river views. This circuit includes sites of early 1900s' homesteading activities, as well as a recent LSCR fisheries enhancement project. For your workout, there is also some elevation gain on both sides of the Seymour River. Starting from the trailhead at Hyannis Drive in North Vancouver, you go down to the Seymour River, around a Twin Bridges–Homestead Trail loop on its west side, then back along the river and up to Hyannis.

From Highway 1 in North Vancouver, take Exit 22 (Mount Seymour Parkway). Going east on Mount Seymour Parkway, turn left at Berkley Road. At the top of Berkley turn left onto Hyannis Drive and park anywhere in that one-block section of Hyannis.

Begin by taking the Hyannis Connector trail at the west end of Hyannis. Follow this trail for 8 to 10 minutes to an unmarked junction with the Bridle Path trail, where you turn left and start along a winding boardwalk. Just after the end of the boardwalk you see on your left a GVRD signpost that marks the continuation of the Bridle Path down to the Seymour River. After about 10 minutes of

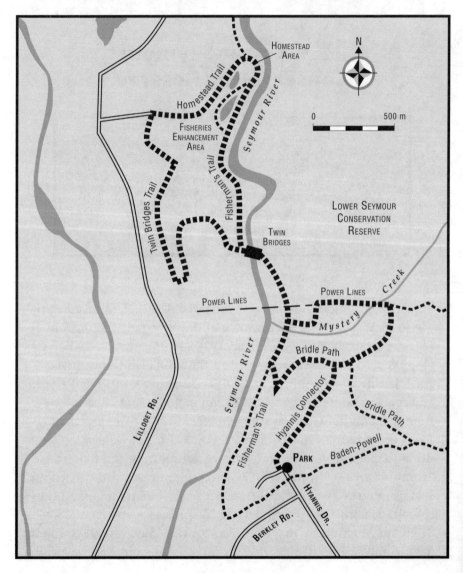

A moss-covered arch from an early 1900s' Seymour River homestead.

gentle downhill on this fine gravel path, you come to a signposted junction with the Fisherman's Trail.

Turn right here, and continue along the Fisherman's Trail for a few minutes until you reach the Twin Bridges (of which only one remains, rebuilt in 2009). Cross this bridge and continue straight ahead up the wide, gravel Twin Bridges trail. In 25 to 35 minutes you reach its junction on your right with the Homestead Trail, near the water filtration plant construction area. A short detour west past the construction area and across the top of the gravel parking lot will take you to a grassy, open area with a pagoda, picnic tables, water fountain and toilets. You next take the very pleasant Homestead Trail for 15 minutes or so downhill to its intersection with the Fisherman's Trail.

Go right here to follow the Fisherman's Trail south, and watch for signs on your left of the early 1900s' homestead activity in this area. The first, after about 100 metres (330 feet), is a small, moss-covered gate, through which an old narrow trail leads about 25 metres (80 feet) to a long-abandoned concrete foundation on your left next to the river. A little farther along the main trail are the larger, moss-covered arches of another homestead. A storyboard there explains how there was a small settlement along the river's edge before the Seymour valley was designated a protected watershed in the 1920s. If you look closely on either side of the arches you will see that several mossy old fence posts, with little round holes for the fence rails, are still standing.

About 200 metres (650 feet) farther along on your right is the Homestead Fisheries Enhancement Area. Some storyboards along a small side trail explain how the new creeks and pools were constructed to provide additional salmonid spawning habitat in the lower Seymour River.

Strolling along for another five minutes you reach an obvious but unmarked side trail on your left. About 15 metres (50 feet) in, partially obscured by brush, there is quite a large, old, brick and concrete fireplace just off the trail on your left-hand side.

A couple of minutes more along the Fisherman's Trail you see a tunnel cut into the rock face on your right. A storyboard explains that the tunnel, completed in 1907, was once used for a wooden water pipeline. It also describes how the nearby pool in the Seymour River was once used to store shingle bolts (long, wedge-shaped blocks of cedar from which shakes and shingles were cut) for the Hastings Shingle Manufacturing Company. On your left just past the tunnel entrance stands one lone telephone pole from those early homesteading days.

Continuing along the Fisherman's Trail for another few minutes you once again reach the signposted junction with the Twin Bridges trail. Cross the bridge and continue south along the east bank of the Seymour River. Note that a small, sandy beach just below the bridge on the east side (when the river is low enough) can be reached by a set of concrete steps on your right.

There are two possibilities from here to return to Hyannis. The first and longer one is the signposted junction with the Mystery Creek trail about 5 minutes from the twin bridge. It is a fairly steep trail and you need to be alert for mountain bikers who may be descending. After about 10 minutes of uphill plodding you come out at the Power Lines trail, where you turn right and continue uphill for another few minutes to the Mystery Creek footbridge. Turning right again immediately after the footbridge will take you back to the Hyannis Connector and out to Hyannis in another 15 to 20 minutes.

Alternatively you can continue along the Fisherman's Trail for another few minutes after the Mystery Creek junction and go back up the Bridle Path trail on which you descended from Hyannis.

The Hyannis Connector Trail in late February.

25 ▸ Mushroom Parking Lot

> **Elevation gain:** 350 metres (1,150 feet)
> **High point:** 500 metres (1,650 feet)
> **Season:** April to November
> **Topographical map:** Port Coquitlam 92G07
> **Hiking time:** 2.5 to 4 hours
> Dog-friendly

A visit to the Mushroom Parking Lot provides an opportunity to experience some of Mount Seymour's fascinating history from the early 1900s. You can combine this introduction to one of the more strenuous sections of the Baden-Powell (BP) trail with other return options to experience a scenic, energetic and varied round trip. The hike takes you from the trailhead at Hyannis Drive in North Vancouver up the BP trail to the historic Mushroom Parking Lot, with three options for your return route.

From Highway 1 in North Vancouver, take Exit 22 (Mount Seymour Parkway). Going east on Mount Seymour Parkway, turn left at Berkley Road. At the top of Berkley turn left onto Hyannis Drive and park anywhere in that one-block section of Hyannis.

Begin by taking the signposted BP trail on the north side of Hyannis. The trail is well marked with orange "BP" fleur-de-lis triangles on the trees. There are lots of roots and rocks on this trail, so watch your footing, particularly if it's wet. Follow the BP alongside

Canyon Creek, going steadily uphill until you meet the Bridle Path trail at a footbridge 15 to 20 minutes from Hyannis. Go to the right here, on the joint BP/Bridle Path trail. At the next signposted T-junction where the trails part, about 70 metres (230 feet) ahead, you turn left to follow the BP north. The Bridle Path, one of your possible return routes, continues in a roughly southeasterly direction across the lower slopes of Mount Seymour (see hike #27).

Soon you leave the stream behind and the BP starts a fairly steep climb, possibly reminding you of tackling the Grouse Grind. After about a half hour or more of steady uphill plodding, the trail levels

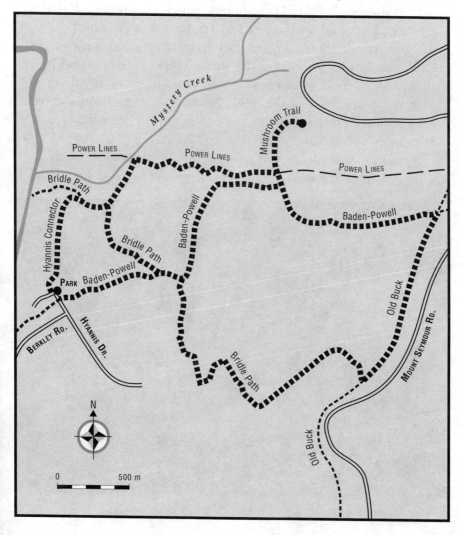

out a bit near its signposted intersection with the top of Severed D (a.k.a. Good Samaritan), a good place for a water stop.

Continuing east along the BP for 5 minutes or so you reach a signposted junction with the Mushroom Trail. Turn left here and you are now headed north toward the Mushroom Parking Lot. After about another 5 minutes you reach a signposted junction with the Power Lines trail. Continue straight ahead into the woods on the Mushroom Trail, which now begins to look more like an old logging road as it heads gradually up through the eerily quiet forest. After 5 to 10 minutes watch for a sign to the right directing you to the Mushroom Parking Lot. Another couple of minutes and you have reached your destination, 1 to 1.5 hours from the start.

The Mushroom Parking Lot itself is now overgrown with bushes and alder, but the original cedar stump still stands, enclosed by a rickety picket fence, and a nearby storyboard outlines the site's history. It explains how in the 1920s the Buck Logging Road allowed vehicle traffic up to this point. A parking lot was cleared and travellers were able to leave their vehicles and continue up the mountain on foot. The Mushroom itself played an important role as an information board where announcements were posted for special

Late April snow at the site of the Mushroom Parking Lot.

events. However in the 1950s a new road was built to the top of Mount Seymour and the Mushroom's usefulness was ended. Along with the storyboard there are a couple of old photographs, one that shows the stump with its original mushroom-shaped cap and its notice board, and another that shows a number of early 1900s' autos in the parking lot.

To return, you can retrace your steps the same way you came up, but there are two other options. Leaving the Mushroom and arriving at the Power Lines again, you can turn right down the fairly steep and rocky Power Lines trail. On your way down you are treated to views of West Vancouver and beyond. Soon you hear Mystery Creek off to your right and shortly afterwards you see the Mystery Creek footbridge, 30 to 40 minutes from the Power Lines/ Mushroom junction. Turn left just before the footbridge and follow the Hyannis Connector, staying on that main wide trail all the way out to Hyannis.

A longer alternative is to continue down the Mushroom Trail to its junction with the BP trail. Here you turn left, following the BP east for 15 to 20 minutes to where it meets the Old Buck trail, once a logging road used by the Buck's Logging Company in the 1920s. Go right and downhill on Old Buck, then after another 15 to 20 minutes go right again on the Bridle Path (a.k.a. Horse Loop on the sign). You are now going west on the Bridle Path, following its red square markers on the trees.

After another 40 to 60 minutes turn left at its intersection with the BP and left again in about 70 metres (230 feet), just before the footbridge, to return to Hyannis in a total time of 1.5 to 2 hours from the BP/Mushroom junction. Another option that adds about 15 minutes from the BP/Bridle Path intersection is to continue across the footbridge and along the Bridle Path to the signposted T-junction where it meets the Hyannis Connector, and turn left there to return to Hyannis.

26 ▸ The TNT Trail

Elevation gain: 370 metres (1,200 feet)
High point: 520 metres (1,700 feet)
Season: April to November
Hiking time: 2.5 to 3.5 hours
Topographical map: Port Coquitlam 92G07
Dog-friendly

On this "trail less travelled" you venture up one of Mount Seymour's lesser-known but quite interesting hiking trails, with the option of taking a few minutes to visit the historic Mushroom Parking Lot on the way back. Starting from the trailhead at Hyannis Drive in North Vancouver you head up the TNT trail, connect to the old Cabin Trail and then complete the loop by returning to Hyannis on the rugged Baden-Powell (BP) trail. Be aware that the TNT/Lumpy Gravy route is somewhat remote and not well marked, so exercise caution when following these trails.

From Highway 1 in North Vancouver, take Exit 22 (Mount Seymour Parkway). Going east on Mount Seymour Parkway, turn left at Berkley Road. At the top of Berkley turn left onto Hyannis Drive and park anywhere in that one-block section of Hyannis.

You begin by taking the Hyannis Connector at the west end of Hyannis. Follow this trail north, passing a signposted junction with the Bridle Path on your right in 10 to 15 minutes and coming to the

Power Lines trail about 5 minutes later. Here you go left and across the Mystery Creek footbridge. At the top of the short hill you turn right, taking that trail into the forest. Follow it for about 5 minutes to a signposted junction with the TNT and NEDS trails.

Just to the left of the NEDS ramps, cross over a large fallen tree to start up the TNT, whose name can be attributed to an old dynamite shack found in the area. Follow the TNT roughly northeast as it gains elevation. Watch for occasional faded red "T" flags on the trees. The trail is steep and rocky at first, then

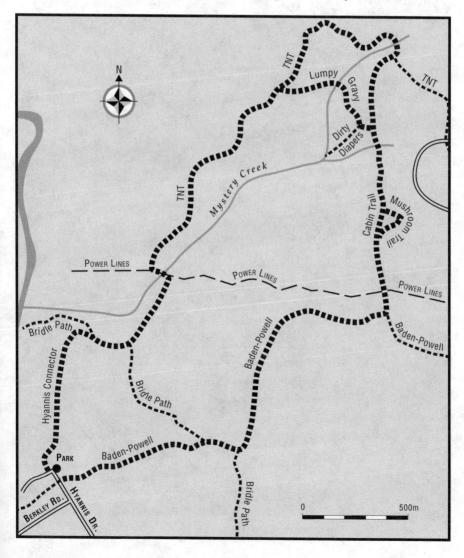

An old corduroy logging road on the TNT trail.

has long stretches of old corduroy logging road, so watch your footing if it's wet.

After 35 to 45 minutes on TNT you reach its junction with Lumpy Gravy, marked by a "To Mystery Ck & Hist. Mushroom Trails " red ribbon on a tree. From here there are two options. You can continue up the TNT trail, enjoying its relative seclusion and following it northeast until it loops around to meet the top of the Cabin Trail (marked by a "CBN00" sign on a tree), at which point you follow the Cabin Trail south and gradually downhill.

A slightly shorter alternative is to go right on Lumpy Gravy, following it due east and uphill. In 10 to 15 minutes you cross a small branch of Mystery Creek. In a further 5 minutes you reach the junction with Dirty Diapers (DD), marked by a "#8" sign on a tree and a large boulder outcropping on the DD trail. Turn left up DD and in a couple of minutes turn right at its T-junction with the Cabin Trail to follow it downhill.

A few minutes later you reach another branch of Mystery Creek with a small waterfall. After another five minutes or so you come to a signpost directing you to the left for the Mushroom Parking Lot, a quick side trip if you have an extra few minutes. The Mushroom is now overgrown with bushes and alder, but the original cedar stump still stands, enclosed by a rickety picket fence, and a storyboard and photographs outline the site's history from the 1920s (see hike #25).

To continue your descent, follow either signposted trail south and downhill from the Mushroom. After about 10 minutes you reach the Power Lines trail. Continue straight ahead for another couple of minutes until you come to the BP trail. Turn right and follow the BP west, passing its signposted junction with the top of Severed D (a.k.a. Good Samaritan) in about 5 minutes. You soon start down a fairly steep section of the BP as it heads west and then south toward Hyannis.

In a half hour or so from Severed D, you reach the BP's signposted junction with the Bridle Path. Go right here on the joint BP/Bridle Path trail for about 70 metres (230 feet), until you come to the next junction just before a footbridge, where the trails part. Here you go left on the BP, following it alongside Canyon Creek for another 15 to 20 minutes out to Hyannis.

27 ▸ Bridle Path Ramble

Elevation gain: 100 metres (330 feet)
High point: 250 metres (820 feet)
Season: Year-round
Topographical map: Port Coquitlam 92G07
Hiking time: 1.25 to 1.75 hours
Dog-friendly

Here is a short, easy, delightful all-weather ramble on the wooded slopes of lower Mount Seymour. This charming trail accommodates hikers of all ages, with several crossings of picturesque little creeks on well-engineered wooden footbridges, and a variety of trail surfaces. The hike takes you from the trailhead at Hyannis Drive in North Vancouver east along the lower slopes of Mount Seymour via the Bridle Path trail, with a loop back to Hyannis along the Northlands Golf Course and Blair Range trails.

From Highway 1 in North Vancouver, take Exit 22 (Mount Seymour Parkway). Going east on Mount Seymour Parkway, turn left at Berkley Road. At the top of Berkley turn left onto Hyannis Drive and park anywhere in that one-block section of Hyannis.

Begin by taking the Hyannis Connector trail at the west end of Hyannis. Follow it north for 10 to 15 minutes to a signposted junction with the Bridle Path trail, where you turn right, go up a short hill and then along a winding boardwalk. The subject of much trail improvement work over the last couple of years, the Bridle Path traverses the lower slopes of Mount Seymour in a roughly south-easterly direction, with lots of ups and downs along the way, but minimal elevation gain.

After 15 to 20 minutes from the Hyannis Connector junction you come to Canyon Creek, the first of several creeks and footbridges you will encounter. Just across the bridge there is a signposted junction with the Baden-Powell (BP) trail. You continue straight ahead on the joint BP/Bridle Path trail, while at the next signposted T-junction where the trails part, about 70 metres (230 feet) ahead, you turn right on the Bridle Path while the BP heads left and north toward the Mushroom Parking Lot (see hike #25) and Deep Cove (see hike #17).

You pass various other trail intersections along the way, but in general keep watching for the Bridle Path signs on the trees. Just under 10 minutes from the BP junction, you come to an obvious

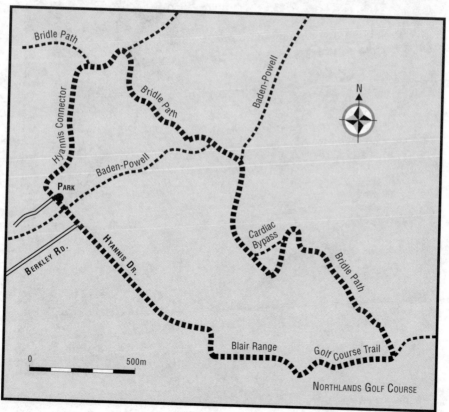

Some recent trail work on the Bridle Path.

fork in the trail, with a pink ribbon on the tree in the centre. The Bridle Path continues downhill to the right, but you may choose to go left on the aptly named Cardiac Bypass, saving yourself a few minutes and a little elevation gain. The Cardiac Bypass rejoins the Bridle Path just before the next footbridge.

About 25 to 30 minutes from the BP junction you notice the Northlands Golf Course through the trees on your right and see a chain-link fence ahead. Just before the fence there is an unmarked junction with the Golf Course Trail, where you go downhill and to the right. Follow that trail to head back west along the northern edge of the golf course for about 5 minutes (watch for errant golf balls) until you reach a large boulder outcropping on your right. Take this trail back into the woods, staying to the left at the first junction and right at the next two, to go roughly northwest for a couple of minutes.

The woods start to open up now, changing from mostly evergreen to mostly deciduous trees. This opening marks the beginning of the Blair Range area, now overgrown with alder but used for many years as a military rifle and machine gun practice range. As you curve to the west along the flat Blair Range trail, you cross the first of three small streams, which may require using a fallen log as a handhold, depending on water runoff levels.

Other smaller trails branch off, but keep going straight ahead and west on the main wide trail. In a few more minutes you see an opening in the trees ahead of you. Here the trail emerges onto a back lane just beyond a chain-link fence and gate. This lane can be a good source of blackberries during August, but you turn right here for a short uphill path that in a couple of minutes takes you onto the east end of Hyannis. Walk along Hyannis for not quite 10 minutes back to where you left your vehicle at its western end.

28 ▸ Mount Seymour Vancouver Picnic Area

> **Elevation gain:** 430 metres (1,400 feet)
> **High point:** 550 metres (1,800 feet)
> **Season:** April to November
> **Topographical map:** Port Coquitlam 92G07
> **Hiking time:** 2.5 to 3.5 hours
> Dog-friendly

After a fairly long slog up the forested lower slopes of Mount Seymour, you can relax at a grassy picnic area, then choose from a couple of options for your return trip, including a stop at the historic Mushroom Parking Lot. This hike takes you from the Old Buck Trailhead in North Vancouver to the Vancouver Picnic Area on Mount Seymour, then back via your choice of return routes.

From Highway 1 in North Vancouver, take Exit 22 (Mount Seymour Parkway). Going east on Mount Seymour Parkway, turn left at Mount Seymour Road. Just after passing Indian River Drive on the right, you see a large Northlands Golf Course sign on the left. Turn here onto Anne Macdonald Way and park either in or close to the Old Buck Trailhead pay parking lot.

Starting up the Old Buck trail, you see a signposted junction after about 130 metres (425 feet), but continue straight ahead on what was once a logging road used by the Buck's Logging Company in the 1920s. After 10 to 15 minutes you reach its signposted junction with the Bridle Path (Horse Loop on the sign), but continue uphill for another 15 to 25 minutes, when you pass a signposted junction with the Baden-Powell (BP) trail on your left. This is where you come out later if you take a side trip on your way back. About 80 metres (260 feet) ahead, you see the BP branching off to the right to head east toward Deep Cove (see hike #17), but you continue uphill on Old Buck. Soon you cross the Power Lines trail and in another 10 minutes or so you reach a yellow gate at Mount Seymour Road.

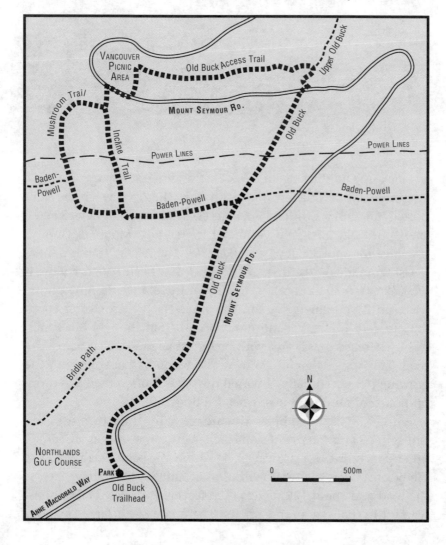

Mount Seymour Vancouver Picnic Area.

Pick up Old Buck again a few metres downhill across the road. Continue uphill for a few more minutes, when you reach the signposted junction for the Old Buck Access Trail. Turn left here, leaving the Upper Old Buck and Perimeter trails up to Mount Seymour's lake area for another day (see hike #30). The Access Trail is a more pleasing, gradual ascent than Old Buck has been so far. Follow it west for 20 to 30 minutes, watching for the orange flashing on the trees, until you emerge at the Vancouver Picnic Area, after about 1.25 to 1.75 hours of continuous uphill from the Old Buck trailhead. There is a grassy area with picnic tables, and toilets across the road. This spot, originally known as Vancouver Lookout until the growing trees eventually obscured the view, is often used as a dropoff point for mountain bikers headed downhill.

After a well-earned break you are ready for the return trip. You can retrace your steps the same way you came up, but there are other possibilities for the way back. Follow the paved road from the picnic area a few metres downhill to Mount Seymour Road. Across the road and about 120 metres (390 feet) uphill there is a signpost where the trail enters the woods. There you see a large Seymour

Trails map, which may help you get your bearings on where you are and decide between two choices for the return trip.

If time permits, you can make a side trip to the historic Mushroom Parking Lot. Follow the fittingly named Incline Trail downhill for about five minutes, turn right at the junction with the Mushroom Trail and continue for another few minutes until you reach the Mushroom itself. The site is now overgrown with bushes and alder, but the original cedar stump still stands, enclosed by a rickety picket fence, and a storyboard and photographs outline the site's history from the 1920s (see hike #25).

To continue your descent from the Mushroom, follow the sign-posted trail downhill toward the BP/Mushroom junction. In a few minutes you reach the Power Lines trail. Continue straight ahead into the woods for another 5 minutes or so until you reach the BP trail. Here you stay left and follow the orange "BP" fleur-de-lis triangles on the trees east for 15 to 20 minutes to the signposted junction where the BP meets Old Buck. Go right on Old Buck and follow it all the way downhill to the parking lot.

A rougher but more direct route back from the Seymour Trails map is to continue downhill on the Incline Trail, listening for bikers who may be coming up quickly behind you. After about 10 minutes you reach the Power Lines trail again. Go left here for about 25 metres (80 feet), then right to continue down the unmarked Incline Trail for about another 10 minutes, when you reach its unmarked T-junction with the BP. Go left on the BP, following the orange "BP" fleur-de-lis triangles on the trees for 10 to 15 minutes or so until you reach its signposted junction with Old Buck. Here you turn right and follow Old Buck for another 20 to 30 minutes downhill to the parking lot.

29 ▸ Dinkey Peak and Dog Mountain

Elevation gain: 100 metres (330 feet)
High point: 1,117 metres (3,665 feet)
Season: July to October
Topographical map: Port Coquitlam 92G07
Hiking time: 2.5 to 3 hours
Dog-friendly

This relatively straightforward North Vancouver hike requires minimal climbing, yet treats you to two quite accessible and impressive viewpoints with a pretty little sub-alpine lake thrown in for good measure. You trek from the Mount Seymour upper parking lot to nearby Dinkey Peak, then past First Lake and over to Dog Mountain before looping back. It is best done in mid-summer to early fall, long after the snow melts and before the fall rains start, as these trails can be muddy and slippery in places at the best of times. In late summer Mount Seymour's ripe blueberries are an additional attraction to consider when planning your hike.

From Highway 1 in North Vancouver, take Exit 22 (Mount Seymour Parkway). Going east on Mount Seymour Parkway, turn left at Mount Seymour Road and proceed about 12 kilometres (7.5 miles) up to the main pay parking area. There is a BC Parks information kiosk at the northwest corner of the parking lot, with a map and brief descriptions of the local trails.

Begin by heading north from the trailhead kiosk on the main trail toward the peaks of Mount Seymour. In about 25 metres (80 feet) a trail branches off on your left; this is the more direct approach to Dog Mountain and is your route out on the way back. Continue uphill, staying left on the fairly steep, narrow, rocky trail rather than following the wide, gravel road on the right. In another few minutes you reach a signposted junction where the trail to Mount Seymour's three peaks continues straight ahead, but you go left on the 350-metre (1,150-foot) trail to Dinkey Peak.

About five minutes later you climb a short flight of stairs to emerge at a Dinkey Peak viewpoint. Although not the summit, this destination has fine views south, east and west over the Metro Vancouver area. To reach the Dinkey Peak summit, only a few metres higher at 1,117 metres (3,665 feet), go back down the stairs and follow the trail to the left for another five minutes or so before climbing to the top of the large rocky bluff with its more expansive

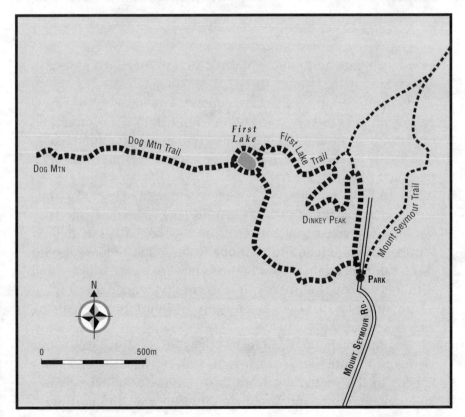

Passing First Lake on the way to Dog Mountain.

views, including north to the peaks of Mount Seymour and west to Crown Mountain.

To continue toward First Lake, follow the yellow BC Parks markers on the trees as they lead you downhill from the summit and back north again to a signposted junction about 10 minutes later. Go left here for First Lake and Dog Mountain along the rather rocky, rooty and often muddy trail.

In 10 to 15 minutes you emerge at charming First Lake in its picturesque sub-alpine meadow setting. The trail circles the lake, but since you go past the other side on the way back, stay right at the signposted junction to continue west around the lake toward Dog Mountain. Again following the somewhat rough, slippery trail with lots of roots and rocks you reach Dog Mountain about 20 to 30 minutes from First Lake, and roughly 1.5 hours from the parking lot.

Dog Mountain, at 1,050 metres (3,445 feet), offers panoramic views of the entire Lower Mainland, Fraser River delta and Point Roberts to the south, and Lynn Peak, Grouse Mountain, Crown Mountain and Coliseum Mountain off to the west and northwest.

Ravens and whiskey jacks may be in nearby trees waiting for lunch leftovers.

When you are ready to return, retrace your steps to First Lake, where you stay to the right to take the shorter route back. At a steady pace you reach the parking lot in another 20 to 30 minutes, or a total of about 45 minutes to an hour from Dog Mountain.

Looking southwest toward Metro Vancouver from Dog Mountain.

30 ▸ Goldie and Flower Lakes

Elevation gain: 200 metres (650 feet)
High point: 960 metres (3,150 feet)
Season: July to October
Topographical map: Port Coquitlam 92G07
Hiking time: 2.5 to 3 hours
Dog-friendly

This rewarding North Vancouver hike features a short, pleasant climb through the forested slopes of Mount Seymour to explore two quite accessible yet serene little sub-alpine lakes. It takes you from the Deep Cove Lookout parking lot on Mount Seymour Road up the Perimeter Trail to the Goldie Lake and Flower Lake area. This hike is best done in mid-summer to early fall, long after the snow melts and before the fall rains start, as these trails can be muddy and slippery in places at the best of times.

From Highway 1 in North Vancouver, take Exit 22 (Mount Seymour Parkway). Going east on Mount Seymour Parkway, turn left at Mount Seymour Road and proceed up to the Deep Cove Lookout pay parking lot just past the 8-kilometre signpost on Mount Seymour Road.

A couple of minutes in from the trailhead sign you reach the first signposted junction, just past a footbridge over Allan Creek. Stay left here and proceed uphill on the old Perimeter Trail. This trail has lots of roots and rocks and in places is more like a stream-bed, but the frequent orange markers on the trees make it quite easy to follow.

About 25 to 35 minutes from the start you notice the Old Cabin Trail, from the Mount Seymour Group Campsite parking lot, coming in on your left. Just after this junction you take a footbridge across Scott-Goldie Creek, which originates up in the Flower Lake area. About 15 to 20 minutes later, you see a small lake on your left as you come to a signposted junction for the loop trails around both Goldie and Flower lakes.

To first follow the Goldie Lake Loop, go right here, then right

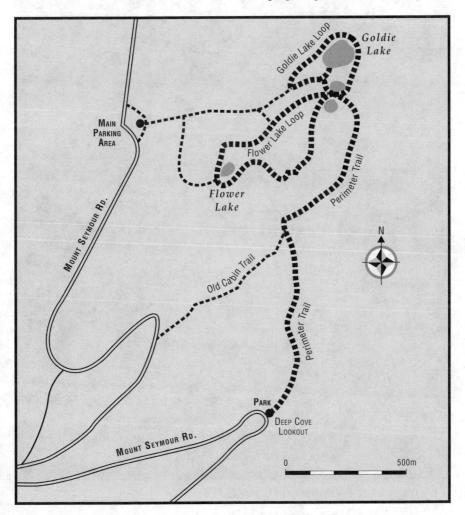

Looking west across Mount Seymour's Goldie Lake.

again at the next signpost about 25 metres (80 feet) ahead. The small lake on your left is not Goldie Lake; you reach it about five minutes farther along the somewhat rooty trail. Follow this trail counter-clockwise around Goldie Lake, about a 925-metre (3,035-foot) round trip. Along the way you find a nice, open, lakeside rest spot on the north side of the lake. Goldie is the better of the two lakes as the spot for a snack or lunch. After your break you are ready to explore Flower Lake, so continue on to the Flower Lake junction.

From the signposted junction follow the Flower Lake Loop trail to the southwest. You can make this 1.4-kilometre (1-mile) round trip in about 20 to 25 minutes. Like the Goldie Lake Loop this trail is easy to follow, but can be muddy in places. Flower Lake is smaller than Goldie Lake and quite reedy along the shoreline, without any obvious places for a rest stop.

Part way around Flower Lake there is a signposted junction for another short trail that branches off west toward the upper parking lot of Mount Seymour. This route is another possible starting point for a circuit of these two lakes, shorter and less strenuous, with little or no elevation gain. If you do start from this main pay parking area, look for the large Goldie Meadows sign just behind the washrooms building and follow the gravel path downhill, with the Goldie Rope Tow on your right. In less than 10 minutes you reach the signposted junction for the two lakes' loop trails. Later, signposts for the Ski Area Parking Lot will guide you back.

Returning from Flower Lake to the signposted Perimeter Trail junction, you now retrace your steps back downhill along the Perimeter Trail to the Deep Cove Lookout parking lot.

31 ▸ Quarry Rock

> **Elevation gain:** 200 metres (650 feet)
> **High point:** 220 metres (720 feet)
> **Season:** Year-round
> **Topographical map:** Port Coquitlam 92G07
> **Hiking time:** 1.5 to 2 hours
> Dog-friendly

On this rewarding, all-season circuit, you venture out to a popular Deep Cove landmark and impressive viewpoint, with lots of ups and downs along the way to provide a little workout, and a variety of creeks and footbridges to keep it interesting. The hike takes you from the trailhead at Panorama Drive in North Vancouver northeast along the Baden-Powell (BP) trail to Quarry Rock (sometimes referred to as Grey Rock), overlooking Deep Cove and Indian Arm.

From Highway 1 in North Vancouver, take either Exit 22 (Mount Seymour Parkway) or Exit 23 (Dollarton Highway). Follow the road east to Deep Cove Road, then stay on Deep Cove Road until it runs into Gallant Avenue in Deep Cove. Turn left onto Panorama Drive and park in the Panorama Park parking lot or as permitted by signs along the 2400 block of Panorama Drive.

You begin at the signposted BP trailhead at the start of the 2500 block of Panorama Drive. This is also the eastern end of the annual Knee Knackering North Shore Trail Run, which follows the

48-kilometre (30-mile) BP trail across the North Shore mountains from its western end near Horseshoe Bay. The trail is well marked with orange "BP" fleur-de-lis triangles on the trees. You first go up a flight of stairs then up a fairly steep stretch before the trail levels out a little.

About 15 minutes from the start you reach the fourth footbridge, signposted as Cove Creek, with wooden stairs on either side of it. Just a couple of minutes, or about 150 metres (490 feet), past Cove Creek there is a T-junction (marked with an orange "BP Trail" double-headed arrow on a tree to your right, and immediately opposite a massive old-growth DNV-marked Heritage Douglas fir just

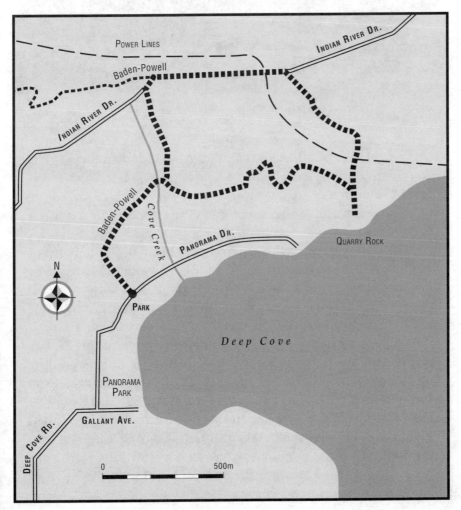

Looking back toward Deep Cove from Quarry Rock.

below you) with a connector trail leading up to Indian River Drive. You could continue straight ahead here to reach Quarry Rock in another 15 minutes or so, but turning up to the left gives you a little more elevation gain and a more interesting circle route approach to the Rock.

The trail is quite well worn and easy to follow, although not well marked other than by some occasional coloured flagging or metal squares on trees. After 10 to 15 minutes of fairly continuous uphill you reach Indian River Drive, where you turn right. A few metres ahead on the left there is a signposted junction with the BP heading west (see hike #17 for a description of this BP segment). Also, the trailhead for the rugged Three Chop Trail heading up Mount Seymour is on the other side of a nearby metal gate. You continue east on Indian River Drive for about 500 metres (1,650 feet), passing under power lines just before reaching the signposted BP junction on your right. Take this trail downhill and back into the forest. In about 5 minutes you reach a wide, dirt road; continue straight ahead to follow the BP downhill at the signpost. After another 5 minutes or so you come out at the power lines again.

Continue south, directly across the open space and just to the right of the transmission tower, to pick up the BP as it heads downhill toward Quarry Rock.

In another couple of minutes you see your destination, the Quarry Rock bluff, in a clearing directly ahead of you. Rest for a while, enjoying the spectacular, 180-degree views of Deep Cove, Indian Arm and beyond. A hundred years ago Granite Quarries Ltd. was located just below this lookout and operated from 1908 to 1924. When you're ready to return, take the BP trail to your left (west), rather than go back uphill the way you came in. At a steady pace you'll be back at the trailhead in a little over half an hour.

ADDENDUM

Two Pemberton Area Hikes— Marriott Lake and Rohr Lake

Marriott Lake and Rohr Lake are worthy destinations if you are looking for an "Off the Beaten Path" hiking experience in the Pemberton area. Both lakes are in lovely settings, surrounded by mountain peaks and alpine meadows.

From Whistler, follow Highway 99 north toward Pemberton, turning right to go east through Mount Currie. The highway, now the Duffey Lake Road, takes you past Lillooet Lake, then quite steeply uphill through a series of switchbacks. About 20 kilometres (12.5 miles) from Mount Currie, watch for the Joffre Lakes Provincial Park signs. Just 3.5 kilometres (2.2 miles) past Joffre Lakes, you cross over Cayoosh Creek and almost immediately come to an unmarked junction with a gravel logging road on your left. If you are unable to turn left here, just over the next rise is a Ministry of Highways maintenance shed where you can turn around, then make a right-hand turn onto the gravel road. There are several pullouts for parking, but the road does become rough, with the type of vehicle you have determining how far up the road you can safely drive.

Follow the logging road north, staying left at a fork in the road, to reach the trailhead in 20 to 30 minutes, depending on where you parked. The trail is rough, steep in places, but quite well marked. About an hour in from the trailhead there is a signed junction where you stay left for Aspen Meadows/Marriott Lake or go right for Rohr Lake.

Marriott Lake

Elevation gain: 400 metres (1,310 feet)
High point: 1,770 metres (5,800 feet)
Season: July to October
Topographical map: Duffey Lake 92J08
Hiking time: 4 to 6 hours, including lunch
Dog-friendly

An alpine hut, the Wendy Thompson Hut, built in 2000 by the Whistler section of the Alpine Club of Canada, is located just northwest of the lake at 1,755 metres (5,750 feet) elevation. Additional information, including a map and directions, can be found at Canadian Mountain Encyclopedia's www.bivouac.com using their Search feature, and entering "Wendy Thompson."

Looking east across Marriott Lake.

Rohr Lake

Elevation gain: 430 metres (1,400 feet)
High point: 1,800 metres (5,900 feet)
Season: July to October
Topographical map: Duffey Lake 92J08
Hiking time: 4 to 6 hours, including lunch
Dog-friendly

Additional information on the Rohr Lake hike, including a map, photo and directions, can be found at the Simon Fraser University (SFU) website: www.sfu.ca/geog351fall02/gp1/hiking/rohrlakeframeset.htm. This map also shows the location of Marriott Lake.

Acknowledgements

Brochures for the Brother's Creek Forestry Heritage Walk and the Lawson Creek Forestry Heritage Walk were valuable information sources for several of the West Vancouver hikes, and can be obtained at the West Vancouver Museum and Archives in Gertrude Lawson House, 680 17th Street. Also, the Historical Photo Archive of the West Vancouver Memorial Library, www.westvanlib.org, contains some remarkable photographs and historical information on the early days of West Vancouver.

The Hollyburn Heritage Society's website, www.hollyburnheritagesociety.ca, and Francis Mansbridge's 2008 book *Hollyburn: The Mountain & The City* were both fascinating and comprehensive sources of historical information for the Hollyburn area.

Available at the West Vancouver Municipal Hall, 750 17th Street, is the West Vancouver District Map and Guide, with its excellent depiction of West Vancouver hiking trails. This map is also on the district's website at www.westvancouver.ca/Government/maps/municipal-map/dwv-municipal-map.htm.

BC Parks has an excellent map with the hiking trails in Cypress Provincial Park, available at www.env.gov.bc.ca/bcparks/explore/parkpgs/cypress/park_map.pdf.

The Pacific Streamkeepers Federation website, Watershed Profiles section, www.pskf.ca/ecology/watershed/index.html, was also a valuable source of background information on the many creeks and rivers of North and West Vancouver.

The District of North Vancouver has two GIS Topography series maps on its website:

Topography and Trails–Grouse Area and Topography and Trails–Seymour Area. They are available for free download at www.geoweb. dnv.org/maps.asp. The maps are both very helpful references, although at time of writing the Seymour map did not yet include many of the trails that are featured in this book.

Metro Vancouver has maps available for areas such as the Lower Seymour Conservation Reserve (LSCR), Capilano River Regional Park and Lynn Headwaters Regional Park. These can be found at www.metrovancouver.org/about/maps/Pages/default.aspx and in brochure form at trailheads in the parks themselves.

In early 2006 the North Shore Mountain Bike Association (NSMBA), www.nsmba.bc.ca, completed an extensive Seymour Trails Signpost Project, during which signposts with maps were installed at major intersections throughout the Seymour trail network. These signposts made travel along many of these trails much more user-friendly for the uninitiated. I personally found them invaluable as I was learning the trails, and would like to acknowledge the ongoing work of the NSMBA, which continues to improve our North Shore trails for the use of hikers and bikers alike.

Many thanks to John Lightfoot of Lightfoot Art & Design Inc., whose many hours of meticulous work produced an amazing set of very detailed trail maps.

I would also like to acknowledge Terry Peters, managing editor of the *North Shore News*, for agreeing to run my weekly hiking column in the newspaper during summer 2008 and again on their website, www.nsnews.com, during summer 2009. Erin McPhee carefully edited each one and managed the process on a weekly basis both years. Without having this reason in early 2008 to continue writing the hiking articles, I likely would never have reached the point of having enough to think about doing a book.

Finally, a major thank you to my dear friend Janet Bowyer, without whom this book would probably not have been written. From 2006 through 2009 Janet and her dog Fritz accompanied me more